Satisfying SOUPS

Homemade Bisques, Chowders, Gumbos, Stews & More

by
Phyllis Hobson

STOREY
BOOKS

*The mission of Storey Communications is to serve our customers
by publishing practical information that encourages personal independence
in harmony with the environment.*

Front cover photograph by Steven Mark Needham/Envision
Illustrations by Brigita Fuhrmann
Cover and text designed and produced by Wanda Harper
Edited by Constance L. Oxley
Indexed by Joyce Goldenstern

❧   ❧   ❧

Printed in Canada by Transcontinental Printing
20   19   18   17   16   15   14   13   12   11   10

Library of Congress Cataloging-in-Publication Data
Hobson, Phyllis.
    Satisfying soups : homemade bisques, chowders, gumbos, stews & more / by Phyllis Hobson.
        p.   cm.

    Includes index.
    ISBN 0-88266-691-6 (hc) — ISBN 0-88266-690-8 (printed comb.)
    1. Soups.   I. Title.
TX757.H59   1991
641.8'13—dc20
                                                                        91-55015
                                                                            CIP

Contents

Introduction

Soup touches something basic in people. It can be a quick pick-me-up or a hearty, substantial meal. Soup in its many variations is the most versatile of dishes and can range from appetizer to main course to dessert with ease. Hot and hearty, it warms you on a cold wintry day; chilled, it refreshes you on humid summer nights.

No other menu item offers a wider selection than soups. Only at home, can you experience truly individualistic soups. This collection of recipes includes homemade, slow-cooking, traditional soups — the soothing comfort foods of the past that evoke feelings of safety, serenity, and well-being. There are also recipes for inventive, exotic, and unusual soups that will delight all cooks — from the novice soup maker to the soup connoisseur.

By emphasizing good, fresh ingredients in classic and imaginative recipes, soups make it possible to serve healthy and reasonably priced meals.

For versatility, creativity, convenience, and nutrition at low cost, nothing is better than soup!

Preparation & Storage Tips

Helpful Suggestions

Use the recipes in this book not as strict formulas to be followed exactly, but as guidelines to be improved upon and embellished. Because of their very nature, soups invite **experimentation** and imagination. Change or substitute an appropriate ingredient or two, or utilize foods on hand. If the recipe calls for carrots, try rutabagas or peas. Try tomato juice in place of milk.

Use your **judgment,** too, in the amounts of the ingredients. If a soup is too thick, add water or stock. If you are fond of onion, double the amount in the recipe. Aim for a **variety** of meats and vegetables, of textures and thicknesses. Try to prepare a new soup each week.

Because the size of a serving may vary greatly according to the size of the soup bowl, the type of soup, or peoples' appetites, the **quantity of each recipe** is given in quarts rather than servings. (Estimate 1–1½ cups per serving.) These quantities are approximate, too, because the amount of liquid may vary with the length and temperature of cooking. **For larger gatherings,** or to prepare large batches for freezing, all of the recipes may be doubled or tripled. For two to three people, the recipes may be halved.

To make **serving** and eating soup more interesting and fun, collect a variety of soup dishes to use with different types of soups. Make soups more tempting by serving bouillon in crystal cups or consommé in delicate porcelain soup plates. Serve gumbo in colorful pottery bowls and cream soups in thick crockery mugs. For a touch of elegance, treat your dinner guests to soup served from a beautiful old soup tureen.

Do not be intimidated by the common notion that homemade soups are labor-intensive and complicated to make. The cooking times may be longer, but the soups usually **do not require constant attention,** so other responsibilities can be carried out while the soup is cooking. Also, soups require less fuel energy to prepare than many other foods because soups are simmered at low temperatures.

Collecting Ingredients

Think "soup" all during the week as you prepare meals. Almost any freshly cooked meat or vegetable can provide an ingredient for the soup pot. **Save the cooking water** and canning liquids from all vegetables and keep refrigerated until soup-making time. (Don't forget to save the vitamin-rich water remaining after blanching vegetables for freezing.)

Learn to **scrub vegetables** well before peeling and then save all the parings (especially from potatoes and carrots), the trimmed parts of asparagus and radishes, celery leaves, and the tops of scallions. Add these remnants to the soup pot for good nutrition and good taste. **Store** all these vegetable scraps and peelings and any vegetables past their prime in a plastic bag in the vegetable crisper in the refrigerator. Label and date all leftovers and **use within a week.** On soup-making day, all these otherwise useless ingredients can be combined in the soup pot.

Meat stock can be made at little cost by purchasing soup bones at a supermarket, or sometimes free of charge from a custom butcher. **Leftover bones** from cooked meats, chicken, or turkey can be used, too. Whenever you get a supply of bones and have a free afternoon or evening, make a batch of stock in your largest soup pot. If you have no need for stock at the time, or if you make a large quantity, freeze the surplus in rigid plastic containers.

Many of the recipes in this book call for vegetables to be cooked and then discarded when the stock or broth is strained off. These vegetables can be used, however, by finely chopping them or running them through a blender or food processor before cooking and leaving the vegetables in the soup for texture and taste. Most of the vitamins, however, are extracted from the vegetables in the long, slow cooking of the stock or broth.

Stocks

Nothing assures the success of homemade soups like a rich, full-flavored stock. So **easy to prepare** and store, stocks are full of wholesome goodness, and depending on how you season, can be **low in salt.** Nevertheless, you need to know how to take advantage of that goodness by ridding the stock or soup of any fat.

To remove fat/grease from stocks and soups. Because greasy soup is high in cholesterol and calories, as well as distasteful, remove as much as possible of the fat from stocks and soups. To do this, yet make use of the less expensive fatty meats, you can remove every trace of fat with one of these simple methods:

1. *For larger amounts of fat,* chill the liquid to congeal fat and lift off hardened fat.

2. Float a paper towel on the surface of the liquid. When the paper towel has absorbed as much of the grease as possible, discard paper towel. Repeat, if necessary.

3. Use a meat baster with a bulb end to suction the grease from the liquid.

To clarify stocks or soups. To each quart of cold soup stock, add 1 slightly beaten egg white and the egg shell, crushed by hand. Bring the stock to a boil, stirring constantly, and boil vigorously for 5 minutes. Then add ½ cup cold water for each quart of stock. Remove from heat and let stand for 5 minutes. Strain through three thicknesses of cheesecloth.

Herbs

Many of the recipes in this book call for fresh herbs. If fresh herbs are not available, dried herbs may be substituted. Dried herbs, however, may have to be placed in a cheesecloth bag, if the recipe calls for the herbs to be removed later. Dried herbs have much **stronger flavors** than fresh, and you may need to experiment to find out the amount you prefer. Begin with ¼–½ teaspoon of dried herbs to replace ¼ cup chopped fresh herbs.

Equipment

Soup pot. For a one-meal quantity of soup, a 4–6-quart stainless steel or enameled pot is ideal. This is the size used in all the recipes. For two-meal or larger quantities, an 8–10-quart stainless steel or enameled pot will hold all the ingredients, yet can be stored easily in the refrigerator.

Cheesecloth. Cheesecloth is used in many recipes for straining the soup liquid and for making small bags, containing herbs and spices for seasoning the soup. One package of cheesecloth usually contains four square yards — plenty for your needs.

Blender or food processor. Most of the recipes call for chopping vegetables. Most vegetables can be quickly chopped in a blender or food processor to speed the preparation process. Or, after cooking, the vegetables may be pureed in a blender or food processor. The possible exceptions are tough or stringy vegetables, such as celery or asparagus, whose fibers sometimes will survive even metal blades.

Metal colander or food mill. Many of the recipes contain the instructions: "Puree in a blender or food processor or force through a metal colander or food mill." If you do not have a blender or food processor, in order to extract the pulp of vegetables and remove the tougher portions, you will need a metal colander (with or without a wooden pestle) or a food mill.

Slow cooker. If you have enjoyed the convenience a slow cooker can provide, you might want to use it often for making soups, since most of the recipes in this book may be made in a slow cooker. Those soups *not* suitable are the cream soups and those soups which require a larger capacity pot. First set the dial on high for 1 hour, then lower the temperature for the duration of the cooking time.

Freezing Soups

The convenience, economy, and good flavor that comes from making soups in large quantities cannot be underrated. The method is simple: Make a full pot of soup, serve, and **freeze the surplus.** Better still, when you have an unexpected amount of spare time, double or triple the soup recipe, then store for use on those days when you have no time to prepare a hot meal.

The following categories of soups, *except where noted* in an individual recipe, may be frozen successfully by completing the recipe, cooling, and then freezing and storing in pint or quart, rigid plastic containers at zero degrees:

Soup Stocks
Clear Soups
Main-Dish Soups
Vegetable Soups
Dried Bean Soups
Fish & Shellfish Soups
Gumbos
Stews
Chili

Not suitable for freezing are the cream soups, bisques, chowders, chilled soups, and fruit and sweet soups, or *any* soup containing milk, milk products, or potatoes as the *main* ingredients. Milk tends to curdle when thawed and potatoes become grainy. If you plan to freeze the soup you are preparing, do *not* add salt and pepper. Season the soup after it is thawed and reheated.

To serve frozen soup, **thaw and reheat,** or reheat over hot water without thawing.

Soup Stocks

Soup stock is a basic ingredient for making many soups. Although a specific stock may be called for in this book, often stocks can be used interchangeably. Soup stocks also add a great deal of flavor and nutrition when used, instead of water, in gravies, stews, and casseroles; in cooking rice or noodles; and when substituted for part of the milk in cream sauces for meats and vegetables.

Because many of the nutrients in the meats and vegetables leach into the liquid during the long, slow cooking, stocks are rich in minerals and heat-stable vitamins. When preparing stocks, include bones — broken and cracked — as much as possible. Bones add valuable calcium to your diet. For flavor and economy, use a variety of meats, bones, and vegetables.

Brown Stock

Yield: 3 quarts

2 TABLESPOONS VEGETABLE OIL
1 POUND LEAN BEEF, CUT INTO 1½-INCH CUBES
5 POUNDS BEEF BONES
5 QUARTS COLD WATER
1 MEDIUM ONION, CHOPPED
4 STALKS CELERY, CHOPPED
2 MEDIUM CARROTS, CHOPPED
1 MEDIUM TURNIP, CHOPPED
10 WHOLE PEPPERCORNS
6 WHOLE CLOVES
1 BAY LEAF
½ CUP CHOPPED FRESH PARSLEY
SALT TO TASTE

In a medium-size skillet, heat the oil and brown the beef on medium heat. In a large soup pot, cover the beef and bones with cold water. Let stand for 1 hour. Add the vegetables. Tie the peppercorns, cloves, bay leaf, and parsley in a cheesecloth bag and add to the soup pot. Cover and simmer 3 to 4 hours.

Remove the meat, bones, and vegetables and discard the bones and vegetables. The meat may be used in other dishes. Strain the stock into a shallow container and chill to congeal fat. Lift off hardened fat and discard. Return the stock to the soup pot. Add the salt. Store in the refrigerator and use within 4 days, or freeze (see page 8).

White Stock

Yield: 2 quarts

3 POUNDS VEAL KNUCKLEBONES
1 POUND LEAN BEEF, CUT INTO 1½-INCH CUBES
3 QUARTS COLD WATER
1 MEDIUM ONION, CHOPPED
1 MEDIUM CARROT, CHOPPED
1 STALK CELERY, CHOPPED
½ TEASPOON WHOLE PEPPERCORNS
1 BAY LEAF
⅛ CUP CHOPPED FRESH THYME
2 WHOLE CLOVES
SALT AND FRESHLY GROUND WHITE PEPPER TO TASTE

Remove any meat from the veal knucklebones and cut into bite-size pieces. In a large soup pot, cover the veal bones, any veal meat, and beef with the cold water. Let stand for 1 hour. Add the vegetables. Simmer, covered, for 3 hours. Tie the peppercorns, bay leaf, thyme, and cloves in a cheesecloth bag and add to the soup pot. Simmer, covered, for 30 minutes more. Discard the cheesecloth bag.

Remove the meat, bones, and vegetables and discard the bones and vegetables. The meat may be used in other dishes. Strain the stock into a shallow container and chill to congeal fat. Lift off hardened fat and discard. Return the stock to the soup pot. Add the salt and pepper. Store in the refrigerator and use within 4 days, or freeze (see page 8).

Fish Stock

Yield: 2 quarts

4 POUNDS WHITE-FLESHED FISH WITH BONES
½ CUP CHOPPED ONIONS
½ CUP CHOPPED CELERY
½ CUP CHOPPED CARROTS
½ CUP CHOPPED FRESH PARSLEY
2 CLOVES GARLIC, MINCED
2 WHOLE CLOVES
2½ QUARTS COLD WATER
½ TEASPOON DRIED THYME
SALT AND FRESHLY GROUND BLACK PEPPER TO TASTE

In a large soup pot, cover all the ingredients, except the thyme, salt, and pepper with the cold water. Simmer, covered, for 2 hours. Add the thyme and simmer, covered, for 15 minutes more.

Remove the fish, bones, and vegetables and discard the bones and vegetables. The fish may be used in other dishes. Strain the stock through three thicknesses of cheesecloth. Return the stock to the soup pot. Add the salt and pepper. Store in the refrigerator and use within 4 days, or freeze (see page 8).

Vegetable Stock

Yield: 2 quarts

2 TABLESPOONS VEGETABLE OIL
1 CUP CHOPPED ONIONS
½ CUP CHOPPED CARROTS
2 CUPS CHOPPED CELERY
¼ CUP CHOPPED TURNIPS
1 CUP SHREDDED LETTUCE
½ TEASPOON SUGAR
3½ QUARTS COLD WATER
SALT AND FRESHLY GROUND BLACK PEPPER TO TASTE
DASH CAYENNE PEPPER

In a small skillet, heat the oil and sauté the onions until transparent, but not browned.

In a large soup pot, cover the onions, carrots, celery, turnips, lettuce, and sugar with the cold water. (Add any leftover vegetables and cooking water.) Simmer, covered, for 2 hours.

Remove the vegetables and discard. Strain the stock through three thicknesses of cheesecloth. Return the stock to the soup pot. Add the salt, pepper, and cayenne pepper. Store in the refrigerator and use within 4 days, or freeze (see page 8).

Clear Soups

The clear soups — bouillons, broths, and consommés — contain the essence of the meats and vegetables from which they are made. They offer good nutrition with fewer calories because they contain only the cooking liquid into which the vitamins and minerals have leached.

Bouillons

Bouillons are clear soups made from lean meats, or vegetables delicately seasoned.

Beef Bouillon

Yield: 2 quarts

6 POUNDS LEAN BEEF, CUT INTO 2-INCH CUBES
1 POUND BEEF BONES, CRACKED
3 QUARTS COLD WATER
2 TABLESPOONS SOFT MARGARINE
¼ CUP DICED CELERY
¼ CUP CHOPPED CARROTS
1 TEASPOON FINELY CHOPPED GREEN BELL PEPPER
1 SMALL ONION
6 WHOLE CLOVES
6 WHOLE PEPPERCORNS
SALT TO TASTE

In a large soup pot, cover the beef and bones with the cold water. Let stand for 1 hour. Simmer, covered, for 2 hours.

In a small skillet, melt the margarine and sauté the celery, carrots, and green pepper until lightly browned. Add to the soup pot. Stud the whole onion with the cloves. Add the onion and peppercorns to the soup pot. Simmer, covered, for 1 hour.

Remove the meat, bones, and vegetables and discard the bones and vegetables. The meat may be used in other dishes. Strain the bouillon into a shallow container and chill to congeal fat. Lift off hardened fat and discard. Clarify the bouillon (see page 6).

Return the bouillon to the soup pot and reheat. Add the salt and pepper and serve.

Tomato Bouillon

Yield: 1 quart

2 CUPS PUREED TOMATOES

1 TEASPOON SUGAR

1 TEASPOON ONION JUICE

¼ TEASPOON DRIED LOVAGE

2 CUPS *BEEF BOUILLON* (SEE PAGE 17)

SALT AND FRESHLY GROUND BLACK PEPPER TO TASTE

CHOPPED FRESH PARSLEY, FOR GARNISH

In a large saucepan, bring the tomato puree to a boil. Add the sugar, onion juice, lovage, and *Beef Bouillon.* Simmer for 10 minutes. Add the salt and pepper.

Garnish each serving with the parsley.

Vegetable Bouillon

Yield: 2½ quarts

2 TABLESPOONS SUGAR
1 MEDIUM ONION, CHOPPED
1 MEDIUM CARROT, CHOPPED
3 STALKS CELERY, CHOPPED
2 QUARTS COLD WATER
1 SMALL HEAD LETTUCE, SHREDDED
2 WHOLE CLOVES
4 MEDIUM TOMATOES, CHOPPED OR 2 CUPS CANNED TOMATOES
1 BAY LEAF
½ TEASPOON GROUND MACE
SALT AND FRESHLY GROUND BLACK PEPPER TO TASTE

In a large skillet, brown the sugar. Add the onion and stir until the onion is browned. In a large soup pot, cover the onion mixture, carrot, and celery with the cold water. Stir well. Add the remaining ingredients, except the salt and pepper, and simmer, covered, for 2 hours.

Remove the vegetables and discard. Strain the bouillon through three thicknesses of cheesecloth. Clarify the bouillon (see page 6). Return the bouillon to the soup pot and reheat. Add the salt and pepper and serve.

Broths

Broths are mildly flavored clear soups made with almost any lean meat or combination of meats and vegetables. Broths are used as simple soups or as a base for other soups. If time is limited when preparing a recipe using beef or chicken broth, excellent quality, canned low-sodium broths may be substituted for the homemade beef or chicken broths. Store the canned broth in the refrigerator. When ready to use, open the can and discard the fat from the top before using the broth.

Yield: 1 quart

If time is limited, substitute two 14 ½-ounce cans of low-sodium chicken broth for each quart of this prepared recipe.

ONE 4–5-POUND STEWING CHICKEN, CUT UP
6 CUPS COLD WATER
1 MEDIUM ONION, CHOPPED
1 MEDIUM CARROT, CHOPPED
2 STALKS CELERY, CHOPPED
SLICED PEEL OF ½ LEMON
1 BAY LEAF
SALT AND FRESHLY GROUND BLACK PEPPER TO TASTE

In a large soup pot, cover the chicken parts with the cold water. Let stand for 1 hour. Add the onion, carrot, celery, and lemon peel. Simmer, covered, for 2 hours. Add the bay leaf and simmer for 15 minutes more.

Remove the chicken, vegetables, and bay leaf and discard the vegetables and bay leaf. The meat may be used in other dishes. Strain the broth into a shallow container and chill to congeal fat. Lift off hardened fat and discard. Return the broth to the soup pot and reheat. Add the salt and pepper and serve.

Beef Broth

Yield: 1 quart

If time is limited, substitute two 14 ½-ounce cans of low-sodium beef broth for each quart of this prepared recipe.

2 POUNDS UNCOOKED BEEF BONES WITH MEAT SCRAPS
2 QUARTS COLD WATER
1 MEDIUM CARROT, CHOPPED
1 MEDIUM TURNIP, CHOPPED
2 STALKS CELERY, CHOPPED
1 MEDIUM ONION, CHOPPED
⅛ CUP CHOPPED FRESH THYME
¼ CUP CHOPPED FRESH PARSLEY
⅛ CUP CHOPPED FRESH MARJORAM
12 WHOLE PEPPERCORNS
SALT TO TASTE

In a large soup pot, cover the bones with the cold water. Let stand for 1 hour. Add the carrot, turnip, celery, and onion. Simmer, covered, for 3 hours. Tie the thyme, parsley, marjoram, and peppercorns in a cheesecloth bag and add to the soup pot. Simmer, covered, for 30 minutes more. Discard the cheesecloth bag.

Remove the bones and vegetables and discard. Strain the broth into a shallow container and chill to congeal fat. Lift off hardened fat and discard. Return the broth to the soup pot and reheat. Add the salt and serve.

Ham Broth

Yield: 1½ quarts

2 TABLESPOONS SOFT MARGARINE
½ POUND LEAN HAM, SLICED
6 STALKS CELERY, CHOPPED
3 QUARTS COLD WATER
1½ TEASPOONS GROUND MACE
4 WHOLE CLOVES
1 BAY LEAF
SALT AND FRESHLY GROUND BLACK PEPPER TO TASTE

In a large soup pot, melt the margarine and lightly brown the ham. Add the celery and cold water. Simmer, covered, for 2 hours. Tie the mace, cloves, and bay leaf in a cheesecloth bag and add to the soup pot. Simmer, covered, for 15 minutes more. Discard the cheesecloth bag.

Remove the ham and celery and discard the celery. The meat may be used in other dishes. Strain the broth through three thicknesses of cheesecloth. Return the broth to the soup pot and reheat. Add the salt and pepper and serve.

Clam Broth

Yield: 2 cups

If fresh clams are not available, substitute three 6½-ounce cans of whole or chopped clams with liquid for the fresh clams.

24 FRESH CLAMS IN THE SHELL
3 CUPS COLD WATER
¾ TEASPOON SALT

Clean the clam shells thoroughly with a vegetable brush. In a large soup pot, cover the unopened clams with the water and salt. Bring to a boil. Reduce heat and simmer, covered, for 5 minutes, or until the shells are opened.

As each shell opens, remove the clams and set aside. Pour the liquor from each shell into the soup pot. Strain the broth through three thicknesses of cheesecloth. Serve. Reserved clams may be served with a butter sauce or used in a baked dish.

Consommés

Consommés are the distilled combinations of lean meats and vegetables and are concentrated, highly seasoned broths.

Beef Consommé

Yield: 1½ quarts

4 TABLESPOONS SOFT MARGARINE
2 LEEKS, CHOPPED (WHITE PART ONLY)
1 POUND LEAN BEEF, CUT INTO 1-INCH CUBES
1 POUND LEAN VEAL, CUT INTO 1-INCH CUBES
ONE 3-POUND STEWING CHICKEN, CUT UP
1½ CUPS CHOPPED WATERCRESS
1 SMALL MARROW BONE
2½ QUARTS COLD WATER
1 BAY LEAF
¼ TEASPOON DRIED ROSEMARY
SALT AND FRESHLY GROUND BLACK PEPPER TO TASTE

In a large skillet, melt the margarine and sauté the leeks until slightly browned. Remove the leeks and set aside.

In the same skillet, lightly brown the beef, veal, and chicken. In a large soup pot, cover the reserved leeks, browned meat, watercress, and marrow bone with the cold water. Slowly bring to a simmer and skim off the foam. Simmer, covered, for 3 hours. Add the bay leaf and rosemary and simmer for 15 minutes more.

Remove the meat, leeks, bone, and bay leaf and discard the leeks, bone, and bay leaf. The meat can be used in other dishes. Strain the consommé into a shallow container and chill to congeal fat. Lift off hardened fat and discard. Clarify the consommé (see page 6). Return the consommé to the soup pot and reheat. Add the salt and pepper and serve.

Curry Consommé

Yield: 1 quart

1 TABLESPOON SOFT MARGARINE
1 SMALL ONION, SLICED
1 LARGE SOUR APPLE, UNPEELED, CORED, AND SLICED
⅛ CUP CHOPPED FRESH THYME
1 TEASPOON CURRY POWDER
¼ CUP CHOPPED FRESH PARSLEY
1 BAY LEAF
1 QUART *CHICKEN BROTH* (SEE PAGE 20)
2 TABLESPOONS COOKED WHITE RICE
1 TABLESPOON FRESH LEMON JUICE
SALT AND FRESHLY GROUND BLACK PEPPER TO TASTE

In a small skillet, melt the margarine and sauté the onion until transparent. In a large soup pot, combine the onion, apple, thyme, curry powder, parsley, and bay leaf. Stir well and add the *Chicken Broth.* Simmer, covered, for 15 minutes.

Remove the onion, apple, and bay leaf and discard. Strain the consommé through three thicknesses of cheesecloth. Return the consommé to the soup pot and add the rice and lemon juice. Stir well and reheat. Add the salt and pepper and serve.

Italian Consommé

Yield: 2 cups

2 TABLESPOONS MACARONI PASTA
2 CUPS BOILING WATER
2 TABLESPOONS SOFT MARGARINE
4 TABLESPOONS SLICED FRESH MUSHROOMS
2 CUPS *BEEF CONSOMMÉ* (SEE PAGE 24)

In a large saucepan, cook the macaroni in the boiling water. When tender, drain and cut the macaroni into rings. In a small skillet, melt the margarine and sauté the mushrooms and macaroni rings for 5 minutes, or until the mushrooms are tender.

Add the *Beef Consommé,* mushrooms, and macaroni to the saucepan. Heat and serve.

Consommé Madrilène

Yield: 1½ quarts

1½ CUPS *CHICKEN BROTH* (SEE PAGE 20)
1½ CUPS *BEEF BROTH* (SEE PAGE 21)
1½ CUPS TOMATO JUICE
2 STALKS CELERY, CHOPPED
1 LARGE CARROT, CHOPPED
2 LEEKS, CHOPPED (WHITE PART ONLY)
SALT AND FRESHLY GROUND BLACK PEPPER TO TASTE

In a large soup pot, combine the broths, tomato juice, and vegetables. Simmer, covered, for 30 minutes.

Remove the vegetables and discard. Strain the consommé through three thicknesses of cheesecloth. Return the consommé to the soup pot and reheat. Add the salt and pepper and serve. This soup may be served hot or chilled.

Main-Dish Soups

Chicken & Noodle Soup

Yield: 2½ quarts

If time is limited, substitute one 16-ounce package of egg noodles for the homemade noodles.

ONE 4–5-POUND STEWING CHICKEN, CUT UP
2½ QUARTS COLD WATER
8–10 WHOLE PEPPERCORNS
¼ TEASPOON ANISEED
1 SMALL ONION
1 BAY LEAF
1 STICK CINNAMON
¼ CUP CHOPPED FRESH PARSLEY
1 EGG YOLK
½ TEASPOON SALT
1 CUP UNBLEACHED ALL-PURPOSE FLOUR
1 QUART *CHICKEN BROTH* (SEE PAGE 20)
SALT AND FRESHLY GROUND BLACK PEPPER TO TASTE

In a large soup pot, cover the chicken parts with the cold water. Let stand for 1 hour. Simmer, covered, for 2–3 hours, adding more water, if necessary. Tie the peppercorns, aniseed, whole onion, bay leaf, cinnamon, and parsley in a cheesecloth bag and add to the broth. Simmer, covered, for 45 minutes. Discard the cheesecloth bag.

In a large bowl, beat the egg yolk with the ½ teaspoon salt. Working with a fork, then with your hands, add enough of the flour to make a stiff dough. Roll out the dough as thin as possible on a floured surface. Let stand for 10 minutes. Sprinkle the dough lightly with the flour on the surface and roll up. Cut the roll into thin noodles. Spread out the noodles on a large cutting board to dry slightly.

Remove the chicken and set aside. Strain the broth into a shallow container and chill to congeal fat. Lift off hardened fat and discard. Return the broth to the soup pot and bring to a boil.

Gradually drop the noodles into the boiling broth. When all the noodles are in the broth, reduce heat and simmer, covered, for 30 minutes, stirring occasionally.

Remove the skin and bones from the reserved chicken and discard. Cut the meat into 2-inch pieces and add to the soup pot. Add the *Chicken Broth* and reheat. Add the salt and pepper and serve.

Chicken & Rice Soup

Yield: 2½ quarts

ONE 4–5-POUND STEWING CHICKEN, CUT UP
2½ QUARTS COLD WATER
1 STALK CELERY, CHOPPED
1 MEDIUM ONION, CHOPPED
¼ CUP CHOPPED FRESH PARSLEY
½ CUP UNCOOKED WHITE RICE
SALT AND FRESHLY GROUND BLACK PEPPER TO TASTE

In a large soup pot, cover the chicken parts with the cold water. Let stand for 1 hour. Add the celery, onion, and parsley. Simmer, covered, for 2–3 hours.

Remove the chicken and set aside. Strain the broth into a shallow container and chill to congeal fat. Lift off hardened fat and discard. Return the broth to the soup pot.

Remove the skin and bones from the reserved chicken and discard. Cut the meat into bite-size pieces and add to the soup pot. Bring to a boil.

Add the rice, salt, and pepper. Simmer, covered, for 30 minutes, or until the rice is tender. Serve.

Chicken & Corn Soup

Yield: 2½ quarts

ONE 4–5-POUND STEWING CHICKEN, CUT UP
3 QUARTS COLD WATER
1 STALK CELERY, CHOPPED
1 MEDIUM ONION, CHOPPED
SALT AND FRESHLY GROUND BLACK PEPPER TO TASTE
3 CUPS FRESH OR FROZEN WHOLE KERNEL CORN
1 CUP UNBLEACHED ALL-PURPOSE FLOUR
1 EGG
¼ CUP WATER
CHOPPED HARD-COOKED EGGS, FOR GARNISH

In a large soup pot, cover the chicken parts with the 3 quarts cold water. Let stand for 1 hour. Add the celery and onion. Simmer, covered, for 2–3 hours.

Remove the chicken and set aside. Strain the broth into a shallow container and chill to congeal fat. Lift off hardened fat and discard. Return the broth to the soup pot and add the salt, pepper, and corn. Simmer for 15 minutes.

Remove the skin and bones from the reserved chicken and discard. Cut the meat into bite-size pieces and set aside.

Bring the broth to a boil. In a medium-size bowl, combine the flour, egg, and ¼ cup water. Stir with a fork, then rub together with your fingers until the mixture is the size of rice kernels. Drop a few at a time into the boiling broth and cook for 5 minutes. Add the reserved chicken pieces and reheat.

Garnish each serving with the chopped eggs and serve.

Cock-A-Leekie Soup

Yield: 2 quarts

3 TABLESPOONS VEGETABLE OIL
ONE 3–4-POUND FRYING CHICKEN, CUT UP
2 QUARTS COLD WATER
2 TABLESPOONS CHOPPED FRESH PARSLEY
4 WHOLE PEPPERCORNS
1 BAY LEAF
1 CUP FINELY CHOPPED CELERY LEAVES
1 CUP DICED CARROTS
2 CUPS SLICED LEEKS (WHITE PART ONLY)
1 CUP DICED POTATOES
½ CUP DRIED PRUNES, CUT INTO SMALL PIECES
1 CUP HALF-AND-HALF
SALT AND FRESHLY GROUND BLACK PEPPER TO TASTE

In a large skillet, heat the oil and brown the chicken parts. Drain off the fat. Remove the chicken and place in a large soup pot. Add the cold water. Tie the parsley, peppercorns, bay leaf, and celery leaves in a cheesecloth bag and add to the soup pot. Simmer, covered, for 1½ hours. Discard the cheesecloth bag.

Remove the chicken and set aside. Strain the broth into a shallow container and chill to congeal fat. Lift off hardened fat and discard. Return the broth to the soup pot and add the carrots, leeks, and potatoes. Simmer, covered, for 30 minutes, or until the vegetables are tender.

Add the prunes and simmer for 10 minutes. Add the half-and-half, salt, and pepper. Stir well and serve. **Note:** This soup should not be frozen.

Chicken & Vegetable Soup

Yield: 1½ quarts

3 TABLESPOONS VEGETABLE OIL

ONE 3–4-POUND FRYING CHICKEN, CUT UP

2 QUARTS COLD WATER

1 CUP COOKED GREEN LIMA BEANS

1 CUP FRESH OR FROZEN WHOLE KERNEL CORN

1 CUP CHOPPED CELERY

½ CUP COOKED CHOPPED TOMATOES

SALT AND FRESHLY GROUND BLACK PEPPER TO TASTE

In a large skillet, heat the oil and brown the chicken parts. Drain off the fat. Remove the chicken and place in a large soup pot. Add the cold water. Simmer, covered, for 2 hours.

Remove the chicken and set aside. Strain the broth into a shallow container and chill to congeal fat. Lift off hardened fat and discard. Return the broth to the soup pot and add the lima beans, corn, celery, and tomatoes. Simmer for 15 minutes, or until the vegetables are tender.

Remove the skin and bones from the reserved chicken and discard. Cut the meat into bite-size pieces and add to the soup pot. Add the salt and pepper and serve.

Turkey & Mushroom Soup

Yield: 1½ quarts

2 TURKEY WINGS (OR BONES FROM LEFTOVER ROAST TURKEY)
2 QUARTS COLD WATER
1 MEDIUM CARROT, CHOPPED
1 STALK CELERY, CHOPPED
1 SMALL ONION, CHOPPED
¼ CUP UNCOOKED WHITE RICE
2 TABLESPOONS SOFT MARGARINE
2 TABLESPOONS UNBLEACHED ALL-PURPOSE FLOUR
1 CUP LOW-FAT MILK
¼ POUND FRESH MUSHROOMS, SLICED
1 CUP HALF-AND-HALF
SALT AND FRESHLY GROUND BLACK PEPPER TO TASTE

In a large soup pot, cover the turkey wings with the cold water. Let stand for 1 hour. Add the carrot, celery, and onion. Simmer, covered, for 2–3 hours.

Remove the turkey and set aside. Strain the broth into a shallow container and chill to congeal fat. Lift off hardened fat and discard. Return the broth to the soup pot.

Remove the skin and bones from the reserved turkey and discard. Add any meat to the soup pot. Bring the broth to a boil and add the rice. Simmer, covered, for 30 minutes, or until the rice is tender.

In a small saucepan, melt the margarine and blend in the flour. Gradually add the milk and cook until thickened, stirring frequently. Add the flour mixture and mushrooms to the soup pot and simmer for 5 minutes, stirring frequently. Add the half-and-half, salt, and pepper. Stir well and reheat. Serve. **Note:** This soup should not be frozen.

Giblet Soup

Yield: 1 quart

3 SETS GIBLETS, CHOPPED (DUCK, TURKEY, OR CHICKEN)
1 QUART COLD WATER
¼ POUND LEAN HAM, CUT INTO SMALL PIECES
1 MEDIUM CARROT, CHOPPED
1 MEDIUM TURNIP, CHOPPED
1 SMALL ONION, CHOPPED
2 STALKS CELERY, CHOPPED
⅛ CUP CHOPPED FRESH THYME
¼ CUP CHOPPED FRESH PARSLEY
⅛ CUP CHOPPED FRESH MARJORAM
½ TEASPOON WHOLE PEPPERCORNS
SALT TO TASTE

In a large saucepan, cover the giblets with the cold water. Let stand for 1 hour. Add the ham, carrot, turnip, onion, and celery. Simmer, covered, for 2 ½ hours. Tie the thyme, parsley, marjoram, and peppercorns in a cheesecloth bag and add to the saucepan. Simmer, covered, for 30 minutes. Discard the cheesecloth bag.

Remove the giblets and ham and set aside. Strain the broth into a shallow container and chill to congeal fat. Lift off hardened fat and discard. Return the broth to the saucepan and add the reserved meat and the salt. Reheat and serve.

Family Soup

Yield: 2 quarts

BONES AND LEFTOVER BEEF FROM BEEF ROAST
2 QUARTS COLD WATER
1 MEDIUM ONION, CHOPPED
2 STALKS CELERY, CHOPPED
½ CUP BARLEY
2 MEDIUM TURNIPS, CHOPPED
4 MEDIUM CARROTS, CHOPPED
1½ CUPS SLICED CELERY
2 CUPS TOMATO JUICE OR PUREE
SALT AND FRESHLY GROUND BLACK PEPPER TO TASTE

In a large soup pot, cover the bones and beef with the cold water. Let stand for 1 hour. Add the onion and chopped celery. Simmer, covered, for 2 hours.

Remove the beef and bones and discard the bones. Set aside the beef. Strain the broth into a shallow container and chill to congeal fat. Lift off hardened fat and discard. Return the broth to the soup pot.

Cut the reserved beef into bite-size pieces and add to the soup pot. Add the barley and simmer for 1 hour. Add the remaining ingredients, except the salt and pepper. Simmer for 20 minutes, or until the vegetables are tender. Add the salt and pepper and serve.

Beef & Noodle Soup

Yield: 3 quarts

If time is limited, substitute one 16-ounce package of egg noodles for the homemade noodles.

1 POUND LEAN BEEF, CUT INTO 1½-INCH CUBES
1 BEEF BONE
2 QUARTS COLD WATER
1 MEDIUM ONION
8 WHOLE PEPPERCORNS
1 BAY LEAF
1 EGG YOLK
½ TEASPOON SALT
1 CUP UNBLEACHED ALL-PURPOSE FLOUR
2 QUARTS *BEEF BROTH* (SEE PAGE 21)
SALT AND FRESHLY GROUND BLACK PEPPER TO TASTE
CHOPPED FRESH PARSLEY, FOR GARNISH

In a large soup pot, cover the beef and bone with the cold water. Let stand for 1 hour. Simmer, covered, for 2–3 hours. Tie the whole onion, peppercorns, and bay leaf in a cheesecloth bag and add to the soup pot. Simmer for 30 minutes. Discard the cheesecloth bag.

In a large bowl, beat the egg yolk with the ½ teaspoon salt. Working with a fork, then with your hands, add enough of the flour to make a very stiff dough. Roll out the dough as thin as possible on a floured surface. Let stand for 10 minutes. Sprinkle the dough lightly with the flour on the surface and roll up. Cut the roll into thin noodles. Spread out the noodles on a large cutting board to dry slightly.

Remove the beef and bone and discard the bone. Set aside the beef. Strain the broth into a shallow container and chill to congeal fat. Lift off hardened fat and discard. Return the broth to the soup pot and bring to a boil.

Gradually drop the noodles into the boiling broth. When all the noodles are in the broth, reduce heat and simmer, covered, for 30 minutes, stirring occasionally.

Add the reserved beef, *Beef Broth,* salt, and pepper to the soup pot. Simmer for 10 minutes.

Garnish each serving with the parsley and serve.

Beef & Dumpling Soup

Yield: 2 quarts

1 LARGE BEEF BONE
2 POUNDS STEW BEEF, CUT INTO 1½-INCH CUBES
4 QUARTS COLD WATER
1½ CUPS UNBLEACHED ALL-PURPOSE FLOUR
½ TEASPOON SALT
SALT AND FRESHLY GROUND BLACK PEPPER TO TASTE

In a large soup pot, cover the beef bone and beef with the cold water. Let stand for 1 hour. Simmer, covered, for 2–3 hours.

Remove the beef and bone and discard the bone. Set aside the beef. Strain the broth into a shallow container and chill to congeal fat. Lift off hardened fat and discard. Reserve 1 cup broth and return the remaining broth to the soup pot. Slowly bring to a boil.

In a large bowl, combine the flour and ½ teaspoon salt. Gradually add enough of the reserved broth to make a slightly stiff dough. Roll out the dough as thin as possible on a floured surface and cut into 3-inch squares. Drop the squares, one at a time, into the boiling broth. When all the squares are in the broth, reduce heat and simmer, covered, for 30 minutes, stirring occasionally.

Add the reserved beef, salt, and pepper to the soup pot. Simmer for 10 minutes. Serve. **Note:** This soup should not be frozen.

Pot-Au-Feu

Yield: 2 quarts plus meat and vegetables

4 POUNDS LEAN RUMP OR CHUCK ROAST
1 POUND VEAL BONES
1 POUND CHICKEN PARTS (NECKS AND BACKS)
4 QUARTS COLD WATER
4 LARGE CARROTS, QUARTERED
2 MEDIUM TURNIPS, QUARTERED
2 MEDIUM PARSNIPS, QUARTERED
3 STALKS CELERY, CUT INTO 2-INCH PIECES
½ POUND LEEKS, CUT INTO 2-INCH PIECES (WHITE PART ONLY)
1 MEDIUM ONION
2 WHOLE CLOVES
1 BAY LEAF
¼ TEASPOON DRIED THYME
8-10 WHOLE PEPPERCORNS
1 MEDIUM HEAD GREEN CABBAGE, CUT INTO SIX WEDGES
SALT TO TASTE
SIMPLE CROUTONS, FOR GARNISH (SEE PAGE 213)

In a large soup pot, cover the beef, veal bones, and chicken with the cold water. Let stand for 1 hour. Slowly bring to a boil and skim the foam off the top. Reduce heat and simmer, covered, for 3 hours.

Remove the chicken and bones and discard the bones. Set the chicken aside. Leave the roast in the soup pot. Strain the broth into a shallow container and chill to congeal fat. Lift off hardened fat and discard. Return the broth to the soup pot and add the carrots, turnips, parsnips, celery, and leeks. Add the whole onion imbedded with the cloves. Tie the bay leaf, thyme, and peppercorns in a cheesecloth bag and add to the soup pot. Simmer for 20 minutes, or until the vegetables are barely tender. Add the cabbage and salt and simmer for 15 minutes more. Add any meat scraps from the reserved chicken parts. Discard the whole onion and the cheesecloth bag.

To serve, remove any fat from the roast and place the roast on a serving platter surrounded by the vegetables. Strain the broth through double cheesecloth.

Garnish each serving of broth with the croutons.

English Beef Soup

Yield: 2 quarts

2 TABLESPOONS VEGETABLE OIL
½ POUND LEAN BEEF, CUT INTO 1-INCH CUBES
1 SMALL ONION, SLICED INTO RINGS
4 STALKS CELERY, CHOPPED
2 QUARTS *BEEF BROTH* (SEE PAGE 21)
½ CUP CHOPPED CARROTS
½ CUP COOKED BARLEY
4 TABLESPOONS UNBLEACHED ALL-PURPOSE FLOUR
1 CUP COLD WATER
2 TABLESPOONS TOMATO CATSUP
½ TEASPOON WORCESTERSHIRE SAUCE
SALT AND FRESHLY GROUND BLACK PEPPER TO TASTE

In a large soup pot, heat the oil and brown the beef and onion. Drain off the fat. Add the celery and *Beef Broth*. Simmer, covered, for 1–1½ hours, or until the meat is tender.

Add the carrots and barley and simmer for 20 minutes. In a small bowl, blend the flour and cold water. Slowly add the flour mixture to the soup pot and cook for 5 minutes, stirring frequently. Add the catsup, Worcestershire sauce, salt, and pepper. Stir well and serve.

Russian Cabbage Soup

Yield: 2 quarts

1½ POUNDS LEAN RUMP OR CHUCK ROAST, CUT INTO 1-INCH
    CUBES
2 CUPS COOKED CHOPPED TOMATOES
1 LARGE ONION, CHOPPED
1 BAY LEAF
1 CLOVE GARLIC, MINCED
3 QUARTS COLD WATER
1 MEDIUM HEAD GREEN CABBAGE, SHREDDED
2 TABLESPOONS SUGAR
2 TABLESPOONS WHITE VINEGAR
SALT AND FRESHLY GROUND BLACK PEPPER TO TASTE
1 TABLESPOON FRESH LEMON JUICE
LOW-FAT SOUR CREAM, FOR GARNISH

In a large soup pot, cover the beef, tomatoes, onion, bay leaf, and garlic with the cold water. Let stand for 1 hour. Simmer, covered, for 2–3 hours.

Remove the bay leaf and add the cabbage, sugar, vinegar, salt, and pepper. Simmer for 15 minutes, or until the cabbage is tender.

Before serving, add the lemon juice and garnish each serving with a dollop of the sour cream.

Mock Turtle Soup

Yield: 2 quarts

2 POUNDS CALVES LIVER, CUT INTO 1-INCH PIECES
1 SMALL VEAL KNUCKLEBONE
2 QUARTS COLD WATER
1 MEDIUM ONION, CHOPPED
2 STALKS CELERY, CHOPPED
2 MEDIUM CARROTS, CHOPPED
6 WHOLE PEPPERCORNS
3 WHOLE CLOVES
1 BAY LEAF
SALT TO TASTE

In a large soup pot, cover the liver and veal bone with the cold water. Let stand for 1 hour. Add the onion, celery, and carrots. Tie the peppercorns, cloves, and bay leaf in a cheesecloth bag and add to the soup pot. Simmer, covered, for 3½–4 hours. Discard the cheesecloth bag.

Remove the meat and bone and discard the bone. The meat may be used in other dishes. Strain the broth into a shallow container and chill to congeal fat. Lift off hardened fat and discard. Return the broth to the soup pot and reheat. Add the salt and serve.

Oxtail Soup

Yield: 2 quarts

¼ CUP VEGETABLE OIL

2 OXTAILS, SEPARATED AT THE JOINTS

¼ CUP UNBLEACHED ALL-PURPOSE FLOUR

2 QUARTS *BROWN STOCK* (SEE PAGE 11)

1 CUP CHOPPED CARROTS

1 CUP CHOPPED TURNIPS

2 STALKS CELERY, CHOPPED

1 SMALL ONION, SLICED INTO RINGS

¼ CUP CHOPPED FRESH PARSLEY

1 BAY LEAF

½ SMALL HOT RED CHILI PEPPER, SEEDED

SALT AND FRESHLY GROUND BLACK PEPPER TO TASTE

FRITTERS, FOR GARNISH (SEE PAGE 201)

In a large soup pot, heat the oil and brown the oxtails. Remove the oxtails and set aside. Blend in the flour and gradually add 1 cup *Brown Stock,* stirring frequently. Add the remaining *Brown Stock* and the reserved oxtails. Simmer, covered, for 2 hours.

Remove the oxtails and cut into 1-inch pieces. Set aside. Strain the broth into a shallow container and chill to congeal fat. Lift off hardened fat and discard. Return the broth to the soup pot and add the reserved meat, carrots, turnips, celery, and onion. Tie the parsley, bay leaf, and chili pepper in a cheesecloth bag and add to the soup pot. Simmer, covered, for 45 minutes. Discard the cheesecloth bag. Add the salt and pepper.

Garnish each serving with the fritters and serve.

Barley Soup

Yield: 2½ quarts

2 POUNDS BEEF BONES WITH MEAT SCRAPS
4 QUARTS COLD WATER
½ CUP BARLEY
4 SMALL ONIONS, CHOPPED
6 MEDIUM POTATOES, CHOPPED
SALT AND FRESHLY GROUND BLACK PEPPER TO TASTE
CHOPPED FRESH PARSLEY, FOR GARNISH

In a large soup pot, cover the beef bones with the cold water. Let stand for 1 hour. Simmer, covered, for 2–3 hours.

Remove the bones and set aside. Strain the broth into a shallow container and chill to congeal fat. Lift off hardened fat and discard. Return the broth to the soup pot.

Cut the meat from the reserved bones into bite-size pieces, discarding bone and fat. Add the meat, barley, and onions to the soup pot. Simmer, covered, for 30 minutes. Add the potatoes, salt, and pepper. Simmer for 30 minutes more.

Garnish each serving with the parsley and serve.

Meatballs & Vegetable Soup

Yield: 2 quarts

½ POUND LEAN GROUND BEEF
1 SMALL ONION, MINCED
1 CLOVE GARLIC, MINCED
2 QUARTS *BEEF BROTH* (SEE PAGE 21)
2 CUPS CHOPPED TOMATOES
½ CUP CHOPPED CELERY
½ CUP FRESH OR FROZEN PEAS
½ CUP CHOPPED GREEN BEANS
1 CUP CHOPPED CARROTS
1 CUP SHREDDED CABBAGE
SALT AND FRESHLY GROUND BLACK PEPPER TO TASTE

In a large bowl, combine the ground beef, onion, and garlic and form into 1-inch balls. In a large skillet, cook the meatballs until browned on all sides. Drain off the fat.

In a large soup pot, add the meatballs, *Beef Broth,* and tomatoes. Simmer for 30 minutes. Add the celery, peas, green beans, and carrots. Simmer, covered, for 15 minutes. Add the cabbage and simmer for 15 minutes more. Add the salt and pepper and serve.

Ham Soup

Yield: 1½ quarts

1 HAM BONE WITH MEAT SCRAPS
2 QUARTS COLD WATER
3 CUPS CHOPPED POTATOES
1 MEDIUM ONION
SALT AND FRESHLY GROUND BLACK PEPPER TO TASTE
1 CUP LOW-FAT SOUR CREAM

In a large soup pot, cover the ham bone with the cold water. Simmer, covered, for 2–3 hours.

Remove the bone and cut the meat from the bone into bite-size pieces. Discard the bone. Return the meat to the soup pot and add the potatoes and whole onion. Simmer, covered, for 30 minutes, or until the potatoes are tender. Remove the onion and discard. Add the salt and pepper.

Before serving, add the sour cream. Stir well and serve.
Note: This soup should not be frozen.

Ham & Cabbage Soup

Yield: 1½ quarts

1 HAM BONE WITH MEAT SCRAPS
2 QUARTS COLD WATER
10 WHOLE PEPPERCORNS
4 WHOLE CLOVES
1 CLOVE GARLIC, CRUSHED
¼ CUP CHOPPED FRESH PARSLEY
3 MEDIUM POTATOES, SLICED
3 MEDIUM CARROTS, CHOPPED
1 SMALL HEAD GREEN CABBAGE, SHREDDED
SALT TO TASTE

In a large soup pot, cover the ham bone with the cold water. Tie the peppercorns, cloves, garlic, and parsley in a cheesecloth bag and add to the soup pot. Simmer, covered, for 2–3 hours. Discard the cheesecloth bag.

Remove the bone and cut the meat from the bone into bite-size pieces. Discard the bone. Return the meat to the soup pot and add the potatoes and carrots. Simmer, covered, for 30 minutes. Add the cabbage and simmer for 15 minutes more. Add the salt and serve.

Ham & Artichoke Soup

Yield: 3 quarts

2 TABLESPOONS SOFT MARGARINE
½ POUND COOKED LEAN HAM, CUT INTO STRIPS
1 STALK CELERY, CHOPPED
1 MEDIUM TURNIP, CHOPPED
1 MEDIUM ONION, CHOPPED
4 POUNDS JERUSALEM ARTICHOKES, PEELED AND THINLY
   SLICED
2½ QUARTS *WHITE STOCK* OR *CHICKEN BROTH* (SEE PAGES
   12 AND 20)
2 CUPS LOW-FAT MILK
SALT AND FRESHLY GROUND BLACK PEPPER TO TASTE

In a medium-size skillet, melt the margarine and sauté the ham for 10 minutes, stirring frequently.

In a large soup pot, combine the ham, celery, turnip, onion, artichokes, and *White Stock*. Simmer, covered, for 1 hour, or until the vegetables are tender.

With a potato masher, mash the vegetables to thicken the soup. Add the milk, salt, and pepper. Stir well and reheat. Serve. **Note:** This soup should not be frozen.

Garbanzo & Noodle Soup

Yield: 3 quarts

If time is limited, substitute one 16-ounce package of egg noodles for the homemade noodles.

1 POUND DRIED GARBANZO BEANS (CHICK-PEAS)
2 QUARTS COLD WATER
2 QUARTS *BROWN STOCK* (SEE PAGE 11)
2 TABLESPOONS CHOPPED FRESH ROSEMARY
1 EGG YOLK
½ TEASPOON SALT
1 CUP UNBLEACHED ALL-PURPOSE FLOUR
3 TABLESPOONS SOFT MARGARINE
1 SMALL ONION, CHOPPED
2 CLOVES GARLIC, MINCED
1 CUP TOMATO JUICE OR PUREE
1 SMALL HOT RED CHILI PEPPER, SEEDED AND FINELY CHOPPED
SALT AND FRESHLY GROUND BLACK PEPPER TO TASTE

In a large soup pot, soak the beans overnight in water to cover, or use the quick-soak method (see page 87). Drain and add the cold water and *Brown Stock*. Simmer, covered, for 3½ hours, or until the beans are tender. Tie the rosemary in a cheesecloth bag and add to the soup pot. Simmer, covered, for 30 minutes. Discard the cheesecloth bag.

In a large bowl, beat the egg yolk with the ½ teaspoon salt. Working with a fork, then with your hands, add enough of the flour to make a stiff dough. Roll out the dough as thin as possible on a floured surface. Let stand for 10 minutes. Sprinkle the dough lightly with the flour on the surface and roll up. Cut the roll into thin noodles. Spread out the noodles on a large cutting board to dry slightly.

In a small saucepan, melt the margarine and sauté the onion and garlic until the onion is transparent. Add the onion mixture, tomato juice, chili pepper, salt, and pepper to the soup pot. Bring to a boil.

Gradually drop the noodles into the boiling liquid. When all the noodles are in the liquid, reduce heat and simmer, covered, for 30 minutes, stirring occasionally. Serve.

Tomato & Noodle Soup

Yield: 1½ quarts

If time is limited, substitute one 16-ounce package of egg noodles for the homemade noodles.

1 EGG YOLK
½ TEASPOON SALT
1 CUP UNBLEACHED ALL-PURPOSE FLOUR
1 TABLESPOON SOFT MARGARINE
1 SMALL ONION, CHOPPED
3 CUPS WATER
3 CUPS TOMATO JUICE OR PUREE
SALT AND FRESHLY GROUND BLACK PEPPER TO TASTE

In a large bowl, beat the egg yolk with the ½ teaspoon salt. Working with a fork, then with your hands, add enough of the flour to make a stiff dough. Roll out the dough as thin as possible on a floured surface. Let stand for 10 minutes. Sprinkle the dough lightly with the flour on the surface and roll up. Cut the roll into thin noodles. Spread out the noodles on a large cutting board to dry slightly.

In a large soup pot, melt the margarine and sauté the onion until golden brown. Add the water, tomato juice, salt, and pepper. Bring to a boil.

Gradually drop the noodles into the boiling liquid. When all the noodles are in the liquid, reduce heat and simmer, covered, for 30 minutes, stirring occasionally. Serve.

Minestrone

Yield: 2 quarts

1 CUP DRIED NAVY BEANS
2 QUARTS BOILING WATER
2 TABLESPOONS VEGETABLE OIL
1 SMALL ONION, CHOPPED
1 CLOVE GARLIC, MINCED
¼ POUND LEAN BACON, COOKED AND CRUMBLED (OPTIONAL)
1 CUP COOKED CHOPPED TOMATOES
½ CUP CHOPPED TURNIPS
½ CUP CHOPPED CARROTS
1 CUP SHREDDED CABBAGE
1 CUP COOKED MACARONI PASTA
SALT AND FRESHLY GROUND BLACK PEPPER TO TASTE
GRATED PARMESAN CHEESE, FOR GARNISH

In a large soup pot, soak the beans overnight in water to cover, or use the quick-soak method (see page 87). Drain and add the boiling water. Simmer, covered, for 2 hours, or until the beans are tender.

In a small saucepan, heat the oil and sauté the onion and garlic until the onion is transparent. Add the onion mixture, bacon, tomatoes, turnips, and carrots to the soup pot. Simmer, covered, for 30 minutes.

Add the cabbage and simmer for 10 minutes. Add the cooked macaroni, salt, and pepper. Simmer for 5 minutes more.

Garnish each serving with the cheese and serve.

Asparagus & Rice Soup

Yield: 1½ quarts

1 POUND ASPARAGUS
1 QUART *CHICKEN BROTH* (SEE PAGE 20)
1 CUP WATER
½ CUP UNCOOKED WHITE RICE
SALT AND FRESHLY GROUND BLACK PEPPER TO TASTE
GRATED PARMESAN CHEESE, FOR GARNISH

Cut the tender ends of the asparagus into 1-inch pieces. (Save the tougher ends for making soup stock, see page 5.) In a large soup pot, combine the *Chicken Broth* and the water. Bring to a boil.

Add the asparagus and rice. Simmer, covered, for 30 minutes, or until the rice is tender. Add the salt and pepper.

Garnish each serving with the cheese and serve.

Scotch Broth

Yield: 1½ quarts

3 POUNDS LEAN LAMB, CUT INTO 1-INCH CUBES
1 TEASPOON SALT
2 QUARTS COLD WATER
½ CUP COOKED BARLEY
¼ CUP CHOPPED ONIONS
¼ CUP CHOPPED CELERY
¼ CUP CHOPPED CARROTS
¼ CUP CHOPPED TURNIPS
SALT AND FRESHLY GROUND BLACK PEPPER TO TASTE

In a large soup pot, cover the lamb and salt with the cold water. Let stand for 1 hour. Simmer, covered, for 2–3 hours.

Remove the lamb and set aside. Strain the broth into a shallow container and chill to congeal fat. Lift off hardened fat and discard. Return the broth to the soup pot.

Add the reserved lamb, barley, and vegetables. Simmer, covered, for 30 minutes, or until the vegetables are tender. Add the salt and pepper and serve.

Vegetable Soups

Borscht

Yield: 1 quart

½ POUND BEETS WITH TOPS
2 LARGE CARROTS
2 MEDIUM ONIONS, CHOPPED
3 CUPS WATER
2 CUPS *VEGETABLE BOUILLON* (SEE PAGE 19)
1 CUP SHREDDED CABBAGE
2 CLOVES GARLIC, MINCED
1 BAY LEAF
2 TABLESPOONS FRESH LEMON JUICE
SALT AND FRESHLY GROUND BLACK PEPPER TO TASTE
LOW-FAT SOUR CREAM, FOR GARNISH

Cut off beet tops, leaving two inches of stem. In a large soup pot, cover the whole beets, whole carrots, and onions with the water. Simmer, covered, for 20 minutes.

Remove the beets, slip off skins, and return the beets to the soup pot. Add the *Vegetable Bouillon*, cabbage, garlic, and bay leaf. Simmer, covered, for 15 minutes. Remove the bay leaf and discard.

Puree the vegetables in a blender or food processor, or force through a metal colander or food mill. Return the vegetable mixture to the soup pot. Add the lemon juice, salt, and pepper. Stir well and serve.

Garnish each serving with a dollop of the sour cream. Borscht also may be served chilled (see page 182).

Cabbage Soup

Yield: 1 quart

1 SMALL HEAD GREEN CABBAGE, COARSELY CHOPPED
2 CUPS WATER
4 TABLESPOONS SOFT MARGARINE
¼ CUP CHOPPED ONIONS
2 TABLESPOONS UNBLEACHED ALL-PURPOSE FLOUR
2 CUPS LOW-FAT MILK
SALT AND FRESHLY GROUND BLACK PEPPER TO TASTE
PINCH CAYENNE PEPPER

In a large saucepan, cook the cabbage in the water on medium heat for 15 minutes, or until the cabbage is tender. Puree the cabbage in a blender or food processor, or force through a metal colander or food mill.

In another large saucepan, melt the margarine and sauté the onions until transparent. Blend in the flour. Gradually add the milk and cook until slightly thickened, stirring frequently. Add the cabbage mixture and simmer for 5 minutes. Add the salt, pepper, and cayenne pepper. Stir well and serve.

Prince of Wales Soup

Yield: 2 quarts

8 MEDIUM TURNIPS, PEELED
2 QUARTS *WHITE STOCK* (SEE PAGE 12)
SALT AND FRESHLY GROUND WHITE PEPPER TO TASTE

Cut the turnips into marble-size balls with a ball-cutter (usually used to make melon balls). Reserve the scraps to use in other soups.

In a large soup pot, cover the turnip balls with the *White Stock*. Simmer, covered, for 45 minutes, or until the turnips are tender. Add the salt and pepper and serve.

Carrot Soup

Yield: 1½ quarts

3 TABLESPOONS SOFT MARGARINE
2 POUNDS CARROTS, CUT INTO ¼-INCH SLICES
2 QUARTS *CHICKEN BROTH* (SEE PAGE 20)
SALT AND FRESHLY GROUND BLACK PEPPER TO TASTE

In a large soup pot, melt the margarine and add the carrots. Simmer, covered, for 45 minutes. Stir occasionally, but keep heat low enough so that the carrots do not brown. Add the *Chicken Broth* and simmer for 15 minutes more.

Puree the carrots in a blender or food processor, or force through a metal colander or food mill. Return the carrot mixture to the soup pot and reheat. Add the salt and pepper and serve.

Green Bean Soup

Yield: 2½ quarts

2 CUPS COOKED CHOPPED GREEN BEANS
1 SMALL ONION, CHOPPED
1½ CUPS DICED POTATOES
2 QUARTS *HAM BROTH* OR *WHITE STOCK* (SEE PAGES 22 AND 12)
2 TEASPOONS CHOPPED FRESH PARSLEY
1 TEASPOON DRIED SUMMER SAVORY
½ CUP HALF-AND-HALF
1 TABLESPOON SOFT MARGARINE
SALT AND FRESHLY GROUND BLACK PEPPER TO TASTE

In a large soup pot, cover the green beans, onion, and potatoes with the *Ham Broth*. Tie the parsley and summer savory in a cheesecloth bag and add to the soup pot. Simmer, covered, for 45 minutes. Discard the cheesecloth bag.

Before serving, add the half-and-half, margarine, salt, and pepper. Stir well and serve.

Potato Soup

Yield: 2 quarts

3 MEDIUM POTATOES, CHOPPED

1 SMALL ONION, CHOPPED

3 STALKS CELERY, SLICED

1 SMALL CARROT, GRATED

1 QUART WATER

3 TABLESPOONS SOFT MARGARINE

2 TABLESPOONS UNBLEACHED ALL-PURPOSE FLOUR

1 CUP LOW-FAT MILK

1 CUP HALF-AND-HALF

SALT AND FRESHLY GROUND BLACK PEPPER TO TASTE

GROUND PAPRIKA, FOR GARNISH

In a large soup pot, cook the potatoes, onion, celery, and carrot in the water on medium heat for 25 minutes, or until the vegetables are tender.

In a small saucepan, melt the margarine and blend in the flour. Gradually add the milk and cook until thickened, stirring frequently. Add the milk mixture to the vegetable mixture. Add the half-and-half. Stir well and reheat. Add the salt and pepper.

Garnish each serving with the paprika and serve. **Note:** This soup should not be frozen.

Cucumber Soup

Yield: 1½ quarts

1 LARGE CUCUMBER, PEELED, SEEDED, AND THINLY SLICED
1 TEASPOON SALT
1 TABLESPOON SOFT MARGARINE
1 QUART *WHITE STOCK* (SEE PAGE 12)
SALT AND FRESHLY GROUND BLACK PEPPER TO TASTE
2 EGG YOLKS
1½ CUPS HALF-AND-HALF

Sprinkle the cucumber with the 1 teaspoon salt. Let stand for 30 minutes. Drain.

In a large soup pot, melt the margarine and add the cucumber. Simmer for 15 minutes. Stir occasionally, but keep heat low enough so that the cucumbers do not brown.

Add the *White Stock* and simmer, covered, for 45 minutes. Add the salt and pepper.

In a medium-size bowl, beat the egg yolks well and add the half-and-half. Add the egg mixture to the soup pot just before serving. Stir well and serve. **Note:** This soup should not be frozen.

French Onion Soup

Yield: 1 quart

2 TABLESPOONS SOFT MARGARINE
2 MEDIUM ONIONS, THINLY SLICED
1 QUART *BEEF BOUILLON,* HEATED TO BOILING (SEE PAGE 17)
SALT AND FRESHLY GROUND BLACK PEPPER TO TASTE
THICK SLICES FRENCH BREAD
GRATED PARMESAN CHEESE

In a large saucepan, melt the margarine and sauté the onions until transparent and golden brown. Add the hot *Beef Bouillon,* salt, and pepper.

Before serving, place a slice of bread in each soup bowl. Sprinkle with the cheese and pour the soup over the bread. Serve.

Leek Soup

Yield: 2 quarts

2 TABLESPOONS SOFT MARGARINE
2 CUPS CHOPPED LEEKS (WHITE PART ONLY)
4 TABLESPOONS MINCED ONIONS
2 QUARTS BOILING WATER
4 CUPS CHOPPED POTATOES
SALT AND FRESHLY GROUND WHITE PEPPER TO TASTE

In a large soup pot, melt the margarine and add the leeks and onions. Simmer, covered, for 20 minutes, or until the vegetables are transparent and golden. Stir occasionally but keep heat low enough so that the vegetables do not brown.

Add the boiling water and potatoes. Simmer, covered, for 30 minutes. Add the salt and pepper and serve. **Note:** This soup should not be frozen.

Onion Soup

Yield: 1 quart

5 TABLESPOONS SOFT MARGARINE
5 MEDIUM ONIONS, SLICED
2 CUPS *WHITE STOCK* (SEE PAGE 12)
3 TABLESPOONS UNBLEACHED ALL-PURPOSE FLOUR
2 CUPS LOW-FAT MILK
1 EGG YOLK
SALT AND FRESHLY GROUND BLACK PEPPER TO TASTE

In a large saucepan, melt 2 tablespoons margarine and sauté the onions until transparent, but not browned. Add the *White Stock*. Simmer, covered, for 30 minutes.

Puree the onions in a blender or food processor, or force through a metal colander or food mill. Return the onion mixture to the soup pot.

In a medium-size saucepan, melt the remaining margarine and blend in the flour. Gradually add the milk and egg yolk and cook until slightly thickened, stirring frequently. Add the milk mixture, salt, and pepper to the onion mixture. Stir well and reheat. Serve. **Note:** This soup should not be frozen.

Spinach Soup

Yield: 1½ quarts

1 POUND CHOPPED FRESH SPINACH
1 TABLESPOON WATER
1 QUART *CHICKEN BROTH* (SEE PAGE 20)
3 TABLESPOONS SOFT MARGARINE
3 TABLESPOONS UNBLEACHED ALL-PURPOSE FLOUR
2 CUPS LOW-FAT MILK
SALT AND FRESHLY GROUND BLACK PEPPER TO TASTE

In a large soup pot, combine the spinach and water. Simmer, covered, for 5 minutes, or until the spinach is wilted.

Puree the spinach in a blender or food processor, or force through a metal colander or food mill. Return the spinach mixture to the soup pot. Add the *Chicken Broth* and simmer for 5 minutes.

In a medium-size saucepan, melt the margarine and blend in the flour. Gradually add the milk and cook until thickened, stirring frequently. Add the milk mixture, salt, and pepper to the soup pot. Stir well and reheat. Serve. **Note:** This soup should not be frozen.

Corn & Tomato Soup

Yield: 2 quarts

2 CUPS COOKED WHOLE KERNEL CORN
1 CUP CHOPPED TOMATOES
2 CUPS CHOPPED CELERY
1 QUART COLD WATER
2 TABLESPOONS SOFT MARGARINE
3 TABLESPOONS UNBLEACHED ALL-PURPOSE FLOUR
1 CUP LOW-FAT MILK
½ CUP GRATED LOW-FAT CHEDDAR CHEESE
½ CUP CHOPPED PIMIENTO
SALT AND FRESHLY GROUND BLACK PEPPER TO TASTE

In a large soup pot, cover the corn, tomatoes, and celery with the cold water. Simmer, covered, for 30 minutes, or until the vegetables are tender.

In a small saucepan, melt the margarine and blend in the flour. Gradually add the milk and cook until thickened, stirring frequently. Add the milk mixture to the soup pot and stir well. Add the cheese and pimiento and stir until the cheese is melted. Add the salt and pepper and serve.

Tomato Soup

Yield: 1 quart

3 TABLESPOONS SOFT MARGARINE

2 TABLESPOONS UNBLEACHED ALL-PURPOSE FLOUR

4 CUPS COOKED CHOPPED TOMATOES

4 CUPS WATER

2 TABLESPOONS CHOPPED ONIONS

½ CUP CHOPPED FRESH PARSLEY

1 BAY LEAF

⅛ TEASPOON GROUND NUTMEG

3 WHOLE CLOVES

SALT AND FRESHLY GROUND BLACK PEPPER TO TASTE

DASH CAYENNE PEPPER

In a small saucepan, melt the margarine and blend in the flour. In a large soup pot, cover the tomatoes with the water. Tie the onions, parsley, bay leaf, nutmeg, and cloves in a cheesecloth bag and add to the soup pot. Simmer, covered, for 20 minutes. Discard the cheesecloth bag.

Puree the tomatoes in a blender or food processor, or force through a metal colander or food mill. Return the tomato mixture to the soup pot. Add the flour mixture and stir well. Simmer for 5 minutes. Add the salt, pepper, and cayenne pepper and serve.

Soup Normandie

Yield: 1½ quarts

2 TABLESPOONS SOFT MARGARINE
1 MEDIUM ONION, CHOPPED
4 CUPS COOKED CHOPPED TOMATOES
1 QUART COLD WATER
1 TABLESPOON CORNSTARCH
1 TABLESPOON COLD WATER
1 TABLESPOON SUGAR
12 WHOLE CLOVES
SALT AND FRESHLY GROUND BLACK PEPPER TO TASTE
DASH TABASCO SAUCE

In a large soup pot, melt the margarine and sauté the onion until transparent, but not browned. Add the tomatoes and the 1 quart cold water. Simmer, covered, for 20 minutes.

Puree the vegetables in a blender or food processor, or force through a metal colander or food mill. Return the vegetable mixture to the soup pot.

Blend the cornstarch with the 1 tablespoon cold water to make a paste. Add the paste, sugar, and cloves to the soup pot and stir well. Simmer for 5 minutes. Strain out the cloves and add the salt, pepper, and Tabasco sauce. Stir well and serve.

Tomato & Barley Soup

Yield: 3 quarts

4 TABLESPOONS SOFT MARGARINE
2 MEDIUM ONIONS, CHOPPED
4 CUPS COOKED CHOPPED TOMATOES
2 QUARTS BOILING WATER
1 CUP BARLEY
SALT AND FRESHLY GROUND BLACK PEPPER TO TASTE

In a large soup pot, melt the margarine and sauté the onions until transparent, but not browned. Add the tomatoes, boiling water, and barley. Simmer, covered, for 1 hour. Add the salt and pepper and serve.

Tomato & Cheese Soup

Yield: 1 quart

3 TABLESPOONS SOFT MARGARINE
1 MEDIUM ONION, THINLY SLICED
2 CUPS COOKED CHOPPED TOMATOES
3 CUPS *BEEF BROTH* (SEE PAGE 21)
½ TEASPOON DRIED OREGANO
SALT AND FRESHLY GROUND BLACK PEPPER TO TASTE
SHREDDED LOW-FAT CHEDDAR CHEESE, FOR GARNISH

In a large saucepan, melt the margarine and sauté the onion until transparent, but not browned. Add the tomatoes, *Beef Broth,* and oregano. Simmer, covered, for 30 minutes.

Puree the tomatoes in a blender or food processor, or force through a metal colander or food mill. Return the tomatoes to the soup pot. Add the salt and pepper.

Garnish each serving with the cheese and serve.

Rutabaga & Cheese Soup

Yield: 1 quart

2 CUPS GRATED RUTABAGA
1 CUP WATER
2 TABLESPOONS SOFT MARGARINE
3 TABLESPOONS UNBLEACHED ALL-PURPOSE FLOUR
1¾ CUPS LOW-FAT MILK
2 CUPS *CHICKEN BROTH* (SEE PAGE 20)
1½ CUPS GRATED LOW-FAT CHEDDAR CHEESE
¾ TEASPOON SEASONING SALT
½ TEASPOON SUGAR
CHOPPED FRESH PARSLEY, FOR GARNISH

In a medium-size saucepan, cook the rutabagas in the water on medium heat for 10 minutes, or until the rutabaga is tender.

In a large soup pot, melt the margarine and blend in the flour. Gradually add the milk and cook until thickened, stirring frequently. Add the rutabaga, *Chicken Broth*, cheese, seasoning salt, and sugar. Stir well and reheat.

Garnish each serving with the parsley and serve. **Note:** This soup should not be frozen.

Italian Vegetable Soup

Yield: 1½ quarts

2 TABLESPOONS OLIVE OIL
2 MEDIUM LEEKS, THINLY SLICED (WHITE PART ONLY)
1 LARGE ONION, CHOPPED
1-1½ QUARTS *BROWN STOCK* (SEE PAGE 11)
1 CUP CHOPPED GREEN BEANS
1 LARGE POTATO, CHOPPED
1 CUP CHOPPED ITALIAN PLUM TOMATOES
½ CUP BROKEN VERMICELLI PASTA
SALT AND FRESHLY GROUND BLACK PEPPER TO TASTE

In a large soup pot, heat the oil and sauté the leeks and onion until translucent, but not browned. Add the *Brown Stock,* green beans, potato, and tomatoes. Simmer, covered, for 30 minutes.

Add the vermicelli and cook for 15 minutes. Add the salt and pepper and serve.

Vegetarian Vegetable Soup

Yield: 2½ quarts

1 MEDIUM POTATO, FINELY CHOPPED
1 MEDIUM CARROT, FINELY CHOPPED
1 CUP SHREDDED KALE OR CABBAGE
1 MEDIUM ONION, FINELY CHOPPED
1 STALK CELERY, FINELY CHOPPED
2 QUARTS COLD WATER
1 CUP ROLLED OATS
1 CUP LOW-FAT MILK
1 TABLESPOON SOFT MARGARINE
SALT AND FRESHLY GROUND BLACK PEPPER TO TASTE

In a large soup pot, cook the vegetables in the cold water on medium heat for 20 minutes, or until the vegetables are tender. Add the oats and cook until the oats are smooth and creamy.

Add the milk, margarine, salt, and pepper. Stir well and reheat. Serve. **Note:** This soup should not be frozen.

Herb Soup

Yield: 2 quarts

4 TABLESPOONS SOFT MARGARINE
1 CUP FINELY CHOPPED FRESH SPINACH
½ CUP CHOPPED FRESH SORREL
1 SMALL HEAD LETTUCE, SHREDDED
1 LEEK, BLANCHED AND SLICED (WHITE PART ONLY)
4 MEDIUM POTATOES, CHOPPED
2 QUARTS BOILING WATER
1 TABLESPOON CHOPPED FRESH CHERVIL
SALT AND FRESHLY GROUND BLACK PEPPER TO TASTE

In a large soup pot, melt the margarine and add the spinach, sorrel, lettuce, and leek. Simmer for 15 minutes. Stir occasionally, but keep heat low enough so that the vegetables do not brown. Add the potatoes and boiling water. Simmer, covered, for 45 minutes.

Mash the potatoes with a potato masher and add the chervil. Simmer for 5 minutes. Add the salt and pepper and serve. **Note:** This soup should not be frozen.

Sorrel Soup

Yield: 1½ quarts

3 TABLESPOONS SOFT MARGARINE
½ CUP SHREDDED FRESH SORREL
1½ QUARTS BOILING WATER
2 EGG YOLKS
3 TABLESPOONS LOW-FAT MILK
SALT AND FRESHLY GROUND BLACK PEPPER TO TASTE

In a large soup pot, melt 1½ tablespoons margarine and cook the sorrel for 5 minutes, stirring frequently. Add the boiling water and simmer, covered, for 10 minutes.

In a small bowl, beat the egg yolks. Add the milk and the remaining margarine and stir well. Gradually add the egg mixture to the soup pot. Stir well and reheat. Add the salt and pepper and serve.

Dried Bean Soups

Navy Bean Soup

Yield: 3 quarts

1 CUP DRIED NAVY BEANS
5 CUPS COLD WATER
1 HAM BONE WITH MEAT SCRAPS
1 MEDIUM CARROT, COARSELY CHOPPED
1 MEDIUM TURNIP, COARSELY CHOPPED
1 LARGE ONION, COARSELY CHOPPED
2 MEDIUM POTATOES, COARSELY CHOPPED
2 CUPS WATER
SALT AND FRESHLY GROUND BLACK PEPPER TO TASTE

In a large soup pot, soak the beans overnight in water to cover, or use the quick-soak method (see page 87). Drain and add the 5 cups cold water and the ham bone. Simmer, covered, for 2–2½ hours.

Remove the ham bone and cut off the meat. Discard the bone and fat and cut the meat into small pieces. Set aside.

Puree the beans and vegetables in a blender or food processor *with* 2 cups water, or force through a metal colander or food mill *and add* 2 cups water. Return the bean mixture and the reserved meat to the soup pot. Simmer, covered, for 1 hour, or until the beans are tender. Add the salt and pepper and serve.

Old-Fashioned
New England Bean Soup

Yield: 1½ quarts

2 CUPS DRIED GREAT NORTHERN BEANS
6 CUPS COLD WATER
¼ POUND LEAN BACON, COOKED AND CUT INTO 1-INCH PIECES
1 STALK CELERY, CHOPPED
1 SMALL ONION, CHOPPED
1 MEDIUM CARROT, CHOPPED
SALT AND FRESHLY GROUND BLACK PEPPER TO TASTE

In a large soup pot, soak the beans overnight in water to cover, or use the quick-soak method (see page 87). Drain and add the cold water, bacon, celery, onion, and carrot. Simmer, covered, for 2½–3 hours, or until the beans are tender. Add the salt and pepper and serve.

Black Bean Soup

Yield: 1½ quarts

2 CUPS DRIED BLACK BEANS
2 QUARTS COLD WATER
3 TABLESPOONS SOFT MARGARINE
1 SMALL ONION, SLICED
2 STALKS CELERY, CHOPPED
1½ TABLESPOONS UNBLEACHED ALL-PURPOSE FLOUR
SALT AND FRESHLY GROUND BLACK PEPPER TO TASTE
¼ TEASPOON GROUND MUSTARD
PINCH CAYENNE PEPPER
SLICED HARD-COOKED EGGS, FOR GARNISH
LEMON SLICES, FOR GARNISH

In a large soup pot, soak the beans overnight in water to cover, or use the quick-soak method (see page 87). Drain and add the cold water. In a small skillet, melt 1½ tablespoons margarine and sauté the onion slices. Add the onion and celery to the soup pot. Simmer for 2½–3 hours, or until the beans are tender. Add more water, if necessary.

Puree the beans and vegetables in a blender or food processor, or force through a metal colander or food mill. Return the bean mixture to the soup pot.

In a small bowl, blend the flour, salt, pepper, mustard, and cayenne pepper with the remaining margarine. Add the flour mixture to the soup pot and cook until slightly thickened, stirring frequently.

Garnish each serving with an egg slice and a lemon slice and serve.

Kidney Bean Soup

Yield: 1 quart

1 CUP DRIED KIDNEY BEANS

4 CUPS COLD WATER

2 TABLESPOONS CHOPPED ONIONS

¼ CUP CHOPPED FRESH PARSLEY

1 STALK CELERY, CHOPPED

1 SMALL CARROT, CHOPPED

4 TABLESPOONS SOFT MARGARINE

2 TABLESPOONS UNBLEACHED ALL-PURPOSE FLOUR

3 CUPS TOMATO JUICE OR PUREE

1 TEASPOON WORCESTERSHIRE SAUCE

SALT AND FRESHLY GROUND BLACK PEPPER TO TASTE

DASH CAYENNE PEPPER

In a large soup pot, soak the beans overnight in water to cover, or use the quick-soak method (see page 87). Drain and add the cold water, onions, parsley, celery, and carrot. Simmer for 2–2½ hours, or until the beans are tender.

Puree the beans and vegetables in a blender or food processor, or force through a metal colander or food mill. Return the bean mixture to the soup pot.

In a medium-size saucepan, melt the margarine and blend in the flour. Gradually stir in the tomato juice and Worcestershire sauce and cook until slightly thickened, stirring frequently. Add the tomato juice mixture to the soup pot and stir well. Add the salt, pepper, and cayenne pepper and serve.

Lima Bean Soup

Yield: 1½ quarts

1½ CUPS DRIED BABY LIMA BEANS
2 QUARTS COLD WATER
2 TABLESPOONS SOFT MARGARINE
2 TABLESPOONS UNBLEACHED ALL-PURPOSE FLOUR
SALT AND FRESHLY GROUND BLACK PEPPER TO TASTE
1 TABLESPOON ONION JUICE

In a large soup pot, soak the beans overnight in water to cover, or use the quick-soak method (see page 87). Drain and add the cold water. Simmer, covered, for 1 hour, or until the beans are tender.

Puree the beans in a blender or food processor, or force through a metal colander or food mill. Return the bean mixture to the soup pot.

In a small saucepan, melt the margarine and blend in the flour. Add the flour mixture to the soup pot and cook until slightly thickened, stirring frequently. Add the salt, pepper, and onion juice. Stir well and serve.

Cream of Bean Soup

Yield: 2½ quarts

2 CUPS DRIED GREAT NORTHERN BEANS
5 CUPS COLD WATER
6 CUPS *HAM BROTH* (SEE PAGE 22)
1 TABLESPOON UNBLEACHED ALL-PURPOSE FLOUR
1 CUP HALF-AND-HALF
SALT AND FRESHLY GROUND BLACK PEPPER TO TASTE
CHOPPED FRESH PARSLEY, FOR GARNISH

In a large soup pot, soak the beans overnight in water to cover, or use the quick-soak method (see page 87). Drain and add the cold water and *Ham Broth*. Simmer, covered, for 2½–3 hours, or until the beans are tender.

Puree the beans in a blender or food processor, or force through a metal colander or food mill. Return the bean mixture to the soup pot.

In a small bowl, combine ½ cup of the soup liquid with the flour and blend well. Add the soup liquid mixture to the soup pot. Add the half-and-half and cook until smooth and creamy, stirring frequently. Add the salt and pepper.

Garnish each serving with the parsley and serve. **Note:** This soup should not be frozen.

Tangy Bean Soup

Yield: 2 quarts

1 CUP DRIED GREAT NORTHERN BEANS
6 CUPS COLD WATER
1 SMALL ONION, CHOPPED
1 MEDIUM CARROT, CHOPPED
1 TABLESPOON SOFT MARGARINE
2 TABLESPOONS UNBLEACHED ALL-PURPOSE FLOUR
⅛ TEASPOON GROUND MUSTARD
4 TEASPOONS WHITE VINEGAR
2 TEASPOONS BROWN SUGAR
SALT AND FRESHLY GROUND BLACK PEPPER TO TASTE
CHOPPED HARD-COOKED EGGS, FOR GARNISH

In a large soup pot, soak the beans overnight in water to cover, or use the quick-soak method (see page 87). Drain and add the cold water, onion, and carrot. Simmer, covered, for 2½–3 hours, or until the beans are tender.

Puree the beans and vegetables in a blender or food processor, or force through a metal colander or food mill. Return the bean mixture to the soup pot.

In a small saucepan, melt the margarine and blend in the flour. Add the flour mixture, mustard, vinegar, and brown sugar to the soup pot and cook until slightly thickened, stirring frequently. Add the salt and pepper.

Garnish each serving with the chopped eggs and serve.

Red Potage

Yield: 1½ quarts

1 CUP DRIED GREAT NORTHERN BEANS
6 CUPS COLD WATER
4 MEDIUM TOMATOES, CHOPPED
1 MEDIUM BEET
1 STALK CELERY, CHOPPED
1 MEDIUM ONION, CHOPPED
SALT AND FRESHLY GROUND BLACK PEPPER TO TASTE

In a large soup pot, soak the beans overnight in water to cover, or use the quick-soak method (see page 87). Drain and add the cold water, tomatoes, whole beet, celery, and onion. Simmer, covered, for 2½–3 hours, or until the beans are tender.

Remove the beet and discard. Puree the beans and vegetables in a blender or food processor, or force through a metal colander or food mill. Return the bean mixture to the soup pot. Stir well and reheat. Add the salt and pepper and serve.

Lentil Soup

Yield: 1 quart

1 CUP DRIED LENTILS
8 CUPS COLD WATER
1 HAM BONE
1 LARGE ONION, CHOPPED
2 STALKS CELERY, CHOPPED
SALT AND FRESHLY GROUND BLACK PEPPER TO TASTE

In a large soup pot, soak the lentils overnight in water to cover, or use the quick-soak method (see page 87). Drain and add the cold water, ham bone, onion, and celery. Simmer, covered, for 1 hour, or until the lentils are soft.

Remove the ham bone and discard. Add the salt and pepper and serve.

Bean & Vegetable Soup

Yield: 2½ quarts

1 SMALL CARROT, CHOPPED
1 CUP FRESH OR FROZEN PEAS
1 MEDIUM TOMATO, CHOPPED
1 MEDIUM TURNIP, CHOPPED
2 TABLESPOONS UNCOOKED WHITE RICE
1 QUART *BEEF BROTH* (SEE PAGE 21)
1 CUP COOKED BEANS (ANY TYPE)
1 QUART WATER
SALT AND FRESHLY GROUND BLACK PEPPER TO TASTE

In a large soup pot, combine the carrot, peas, tomato, turnip, rice, and *Beef Broth*. Simmer, covered, for 35–45 minutes, or until the rice is cooked and the vegetables are tender.

Add the beans, water, salt, and pepper. Reheat and serve.

Bean & Tomato Soup

Yield: 2½ quarts

2 CUPS DRIED NAVY BEANS
5 CUPS COLD WATER
2 CUPS COOKED CHOPPED TOMATOES
1 CLOVE GARLIC, CUT IN HALF LENGTHWISE
8–10 WHOLE PEPPERCORNS
1 BAY LEAF
½ CUP CHOPPED FRESH PARSLEY
¼ TEASPOON DRIED MARJORAM
½ CUP CHOPPED ONIONS
SALT AND FRESHLY GROUND BLACK PEPPER TO TASTE

In a large soup pot, soak the beans overnight in water to cover, or use the quick-soak method (see page 87). Drain and add the cold water and tomatoes. Simmer, covered, for 3 hours, or until the beans are tender. Tie the garlic, peppercorns, bay leaf, parsley, marjoram, and onions in a cheesecloth bag and add to the soup pot. Simmer, covered, for 30 minutes. Discard the cheesecloth bag.

Puree the beans and vegetables in a blender or food processor, or force through a metal colander or food mill. Return the bean mixture to the soup pot. Stir well and reheat. Add the salt and pepper and serve.

Bean & Spinach Soup

Yield: 2 quarts

1 CUP DRIED NAVY BEANS
2 QUARTS *WHITE STOCK* (SEE PAGE 12)
1 BAY LEAF
1 MEDIUM ONION, CHOPPED
1 CLOVE GARLIC, MINCED
2 TABLESPOONS SOFT MARGARINE
1 TABLESPOON UNBLEACHED ALL-PURPOSE FLOUR
2 CUPS COOKED CHOPPED SPINACH
SALT AND FRESHLY GROUND BLACK PEPPER TO TASTE

In a large soup pot, soak the beans overnight in water to cover, or use the quick-soak method (see page 87). Drain and add the *White Stock,* bay leaf, onion, and garlic. Simmer, covered, for 3–3½ hours, or until the beans are tender.

Puree the beans and vegetables in a blender or food processor, or force through a metal colander or food mill. Return the bean mixture to the soup pot.

In a small saucepan, melt the margarine and blend in the flour. Add ⅛ cup of the soup liquid and blend. Add the soup liquid mixture to the soup pot and cook until slightly thickened, stirring frequently.

Remove the bay leaf and discard. Add the spinach, salt, and pepper. Reheat and serve.

Bean & Meatball Soup

Yield: 2 quarts

2 CUPS DRIED PINTO BEANS
2 QUARTS *BEEF BROTH* (SEE PAGE 21)
1 MEDIUM ONION, CHOPPED
2 CLOVES GARLIC, MINCED
1 STALK CELERY, CHOPPED
2 MEDIUM CARROTS, CHOPPED
2 CUPS COOKED CHOPPED TOMATOES
MEATBALLS (SEE RECIPE BELOW)
1½ CUPS SHREDDED CABBAGE
SALT AND FRESHLY GROUND BLACK PEPPER TO TASTE

In a large soup pot, soak the beans overnight in water to cover, or use the quick-soak method (see page 87). Drain and add the *Beef Broth,* onion, and garlic. Simmer, covered, for 2–2½ hours, or until the beans are tender.

Add the celery, carrots, tomatoes, and meatballs. Simmer, covered, for 30 minutes, or until the vegetables are tender. Add the cabbage and cook for 10 minutes, or until the cabbage is tender crisp. Add the salt and pepper and serve.

Meatballs:
1 POUND LEAN GROUND BEEF
¼ CUP MINCED ONIONS
2 TABLESPOONS CHOPPED FRESH PARSLEY
1 EGG
¼ CUP DRY BREAD CRUMBS
⅛ TEASPOON FRESHLY GROUND BLACK PEPPER
¼ TEASPOON DRIED OREGANO
2 TABLESPOONS VEGETABLE OIL

In a medium-size bowl, mix together all the ingredients and shape into 24 small meatballs. In a large skillet, heat the oil and brown the meatballs. Drain off the fat and add the meatballs to the soup.

Bean & Cheese Soup

Yield: 1½ quarts

1 STALK CELERY, CHOPPED

1 SMALL CARROT, CHOPPED

1 SMALL GREEN BELL PEPPER, CORED, SEEDED, AND CHOPPED

1 CUP WATER

¼ CUP SOFT MARGARINE

¼ CUP UNBLEACHED ALL-PURPOSE FLOUR

1 QUART *CHICKEN BROTH* (SEE PAGE 20)

½ CUP GRATED LOW-FAT CHEDDAR CHEESE

1 CUP COOKED GREAT NORTHERN OR NAVY BEANS

SALT AND FRESHLY GROUND BLACK PEPPER TO TASTE

In a large saucepan, cook the vegetables in the water on medium heat for 1 hour, or until the vegetables are tender.

In a large soup pot, melt the margarine and blend in the flour. Gradually add the *Chicken Broth* and cook until slightly thickened, stirring frequently. Add the cheese and blend well.

Puree the vegetables and beans in a blender or food processor, or force through a metal colander or food mill. Add the vegetable mixture to the cheese mixture. Stir well and reheat. Add the salt and pepper and serve.

Bean & Pea Soup

Yield: 3 quarts

1 CUP DRIED PINTO BEANS
1 CUP DRIED NAVY BEANS
2 CUPS DRIED SPLIT PEAS
3½ QUARTS COLD WATER
8 WHOLE PEPPERCORNS
1 HAM BONE WITH MEAT SCRAPS
3 STALKS CELERY, CHOPPED
2 SMALL ONIONS, THINLY SLICED
3 MEDIUM CARROTS, DICED
¼ TEASPOON GROUND MUSTARD
SALT TO TASTE

In a large soup pot, soak the beans and peas overnight in water to cover, or use the quick-soak method (see page 87). Drain and add the cold water. Tie the peppercorns in a cheesecloth bag and add to the soup pot. Add all the remaining ingredients, except the salt. Simmer, covered, for 3–3½ hours, or until the beans and peas are tender. Discard the cheesecloth bag.

Remove the ham bone and cut off the meat. Discard the bone and fat and cut the meat into small pieces. Set aside.

Puree the beans, peas, and vegetables in a blender or food processor, or force through a metal colander or food mill. Return the bean mixture and the reserved meat to the soup pot. Stir well and reheat. Add the salt and serve.

Split Pea Soup

Yield: 2 quarts

1 CUP DRIED SPLIT PEAS
3 QUARTS COLD WATER
1 HAM BONE
1 TABLESPOON CHOPPED ONIONS
3 TABLESPOONS SOFT MARGARINE
3 TABLESPOONS UNBLEACHED ALL-PURPOSE FLOUR
2 CUPS LOW-FAT MILK
SALT AND FRESHLY GROUND BLACK PEPPER TO TASTE

In a large soup pot, soak the peas overnight in water to cover, or use the quick-soak method (see page 87). Drain and add the cold water, ham bone, and onions. Simmer, covered, for 1–1½ hours, or until the peas are soft.

In a small saucepan, melt the margarine and blend in the flour. Add ⅛ cup of the soup liquid and stir until well blended. Add the soup liquid mixture and the milk to the soup pot and cook until slightly thickened, stirring frequently. Remove the ham bone and discard. Add the salt and pepper and serve. **Note:** This soup should not be frozen.

Pea & Tomato Soup

Yield: 1 quart

1 CUP DRIED YELLOW SPLIT PEAS
4 CUPS COLD WATER
2 CUPS CHOPPED TOMATOES
1 MEDIUM ONION, CHOPPED
1 STALK CELERY, CHOPPED
SALT AND FRESHLY GROUND BLACK PEPPER TO TASTE
LEMON SLICES, FOR GARNISH

In a large soup pot, soak the peas overnight in water to cover, or use the quick-soak method (see page 87). Drain and add the cold water, tomatoes, onion, and celery. Simmer, covered, for 1–1½ hours, or until the peas are soft.

Puree the vegetables in a blender or food processor, or force through a metal colander or food mill. Return the vegetable mixture to the soup pot. Stir well and reheat. Add the salt and pepper.

Garnish each serving with a lemon slice and serve.

The Quick-Soak Method

The quick-soak method is good to use when time is limited or when you haven't planned ahead to soak dried beans or peas overnight.

In a large soup pot, cover the beans or peas with water. Bring to a boil and cook, covered, for 2 minutes. Remove the pot from the heat and let stand for 1–2 hours. This is equivalent to as much as 15 hours of soaking time.

Cream Soups

Cream soups are not suitable for freezing.

Cream of Artichoke Soup

Yield: 1½ quarts

2 CUPS PEELED AND CHOPPED JERUSALEM ARTICHOKES
1 TABLESPOON MINCED ONIONS
3 CUPS WATER
2 TABLESPOONS SOFT MARGARINE
2 TABLESPOONS UNBLEACHED ALL-PURPOSE FLOUR
2 CUPS LOW-FAT MILK
1 EGG, BEATEN
SALT AND FRESHLY GROUND BLACK PEPPER TO TASTE
DASH CAYENNE PEPPER

In a large soup pot, cook the artichokes and onions in the water on medium heat for 30 minutes, or until the artichokes are tender. Drain and reserve the cooking liquid in the soup pot.

Puree the vegetables in a blender or food processor, or force through a metal colander or food mill. Return the vegetables to the soup pot.

In a medium-size saucepan, melt the margarine and blend in the flour. Gradually add the milk and cook until slightly thickened, stirring frequently. Add the egg and cook until thickened. Add the egg mixture to the vegetable mixture. Stir well and reheat. Add the salt, pepper, and cayenne pepper and serve.

Cream of Asparagus Soup

Yield: 2 quarts

2 POUNDS ASPARAGUS, CHOPPED
¼ CUP CHOPPED ONIONS
½ CUP CHOPPED CELERY
4 CUPS WATER
3 TABLESPOONS SOFT MARGARINE
3 TABLESPOONS UNBLEACHED ALL-PURPOSE FLOUR
½ CUP HALF-AND-HALF
2 CUPS *CHICKEN BROTH* (SEE PAGE 20)
SALT AND FRESHLY GROUND BLACK PEPPER TO TASTE

In a large soup pot, cook the asparagus, onions, and celery in the water on medium heat for 20–30 minutes, or until the vegetables are tender. Drain and reserve the cooking liquid in the soup pot.

Puree the vegetables in a blender or food processor, or force through a metal colander or food mill. Return the vegetables to the soup pot.

In a large saucepan, melt the margarine and blend in the flour. Gradually add the half-and-half and cook until thickened, stirring frequently. Add the *Chicken Broth* and stir well. Add the *Chicken Broth* mixture to the vegetable mixture and simmer for 5 minutes. Add the salt and pepper and serve.

Cream of Carrot Soup

Yield: 1½ quarts

4 LARGE CARROTS, SLICED
2 CUPS WATER
3 TABLESPOONS SOFT MARGARINE
3 TABLESPOONS UNBLEACHED ALL-PURPOSE FLOUR
3½ CUPS LOW-FAT MILK
SALT AND FRESHLY GROUND BLACK PEPPER TO TASTE

In a large soup pot, cook the carrots in the water on medium heat for 15 minutes, or until the carrots are tender. Drain and reserve the cooking liquid in the soup pot.

Puree the carrots in a blender or food processor, or force through a metal colander or food mill. Return the carrots to the soup pot.

In a large saucepan, melt the margarine and blend in the flour. Gradually add the milk and cook until thickened, stirring frequently. Add the milk mixture to the carrot mixture. Stir well and reheat. Add the salt and pepper and serve.

Cream of Cauliflower Soup

Yield: 1½ quarts

1 MEDIUM CAULIFLOWER, COARSELY CHOPPED
4 CUPS WATER
4 TABLESPOONS SOFT MARGARINE
3 TABLESPOONS CHOPPED ONIONS
4 TABLESPOONS UNBLEACHED ALL-PURPOSE FLOUR
2 CUPS LOW-FAT MILK
3 TABLESPOONS GRATED LOW-FAT CHEDDAR CHEESE
1 EGG YOLK
SALT AND FRESHLY GROUND BLACK PEPPER TO TASTE

In a large soup pot, cook the cauliflower in the water on medium heat for 15 minutes, or until the cauliflower is tender. Drain and reserve the cooking liquid in the soup pot.

Puree the cauliflower in a blender or food processor, or force through a metal colander or food mill. Return the cauliflower to the soup pot.

In a medium-size saucepan, melt the margarine and sauté the onions until transparent. Blend in the flour. Gradually add the milk and cook until thickened, stirring frequently. Add the cheese and egg yolk and cook until the cheese is melted. Add the cheese mixture to the cauliflower mixture. Stir well and reheat. Add the salt and pepper and serve.

Cream of Celeriac Soup

Yield: 1½ quarts

4 CUPS PEELED AND CHOPPED CELERIAC
4 CUPS *WHITE STOCK* OR *CHICKEN BROTH* (SEE PAGES 12
   AND 20)
2 TABLESPOONS SOFT MARGARINE
1 TABLESPOON UNBLEACHED ALL-PURPOSE FLOUR
1 CUP HALF-AND-HALF
SALT AND FRESHLY GROUND BLACK PEPPER TO TASTE

In a large soup pot, cook the celeriac in the *White Stock* on medium heat for 30 minutes, or until the celeriac is tender. Drain and reserve the cooking liquid in the soup pot.

Puree the celeriac in a blender or food processor, or force through a metal colander or food mill. Return the celeriac to the soup pot.

In a small saucepan, melt the margarine and blend in the flour. Gradually add the half-and-half and cook until thickened, stirring frequently. Add the half-and-half mixture to the celeriac mixture. Stir well and reheat. Add the salt and pepper and serve.

Celeriac is appearing in produce departments across the country. It is a knobby and mottled-looking vegetable with a mild celery taste and a firm texture. Use it raw in salads or in any cooked dish. To use raw, always peel celeriac and blanch briefly.

Cream of Celery Soup

Yield: 1½ quarts

2 CUPS CHOPPED CELERY
1 TABLESPOON CHOPPED GREEN BELL PEPPER
2 CUPS *WHITE STOCK* (SEE PAGE 12)
1 TABLESPOON SOFT MARGARINE
1 TABLESPOON UNBLEACHED ALL-PURPOSE FLOUR
1 CUP LOW-FAT MILK
¾ CUP HALF-AND-HALF
SALT AND FRESHLY GROUND BLACK PEPPER TO TASTE

In a large soup pot, cook the celery and green pepper in the *White Stock* on medium heat for 30 minutes, or until the vegetables are tender. Drain and reserve the cooking liquid in the soup pot.

Puree the vegetables in a blender or food processor, or force through a metal colander or food mill. Return the vegetables to the soup pot.

In a small saucepan, melt the margarine and blend in the flour. Gradually add enough soup liquid to make a smooth paste. Add the paste to the soup pot and simmer until smooth and thickened, stirring frequently. Add the milk and half-and-half. Stir well and reheat. Add the salt and pepper and serve.

Cream of Cheese Soup

Yield: 1 quart

4 TABLESPOONS SOFT MARGARINE
¼ CUP MINCED ONIONS
4 TABLESPOONS UNBLEACHED ALL-PURPOSE FLOUR
4 CUPS LOW-FAT MILK
1 CUP GRATED SWISS CHEESE
½ CUP COOKED PEAS
¼ CUP CHOPPED RED BELL PEPPER
SALT AND FRESHLY GROUND BLACK PEPPER TO TASTE

In a large saucepan, melt the margarine and sauté the onions until transparent. Blend in the flour. Gradually add 2 cups milk and cook until thickened, stirring frequently. Add the remaining milk and blend well.

Add the cheese and cook until the cheese is melted. Add the peas and bell pepper and cook for 5 minutes. Add the salt and pepper and serve.

Cream of Chestnut Soup

Yield: 1 quart

4 CUPS SHELLED AND BLANCHED CHESTNUTS
2 CUPS *WHITE STOCK* OR *CHICKEN BROTH* (SEE PAGES 12
    AND 20)
2 TABLESPOONS SOFT MARGARINE
2 TABLESPOONS UNBLEACHED ALL-PURPOSE FLOUR
2 CUPS LOW-FAT MILK
SALT AND FRESHLY GROUND BLACK PEPPER TO TASTE

In a large saucepan, cook the chestnuts in the *White Stock* on medium heat for 20 minutes, or until the chestnuts are soft. Drain and reserve the cooking liquid in the saucepan.

Puree the chestnuts in a blender or food processor, or force through a metal colander or food mill. Return the chestnuts to the saucepan.

In a medium-size saucepan, melt the margarine and blend in the flour. Gradually add the milk and cook until thickened, stirring frequently. Add the milk mixture to the chestnut mixture. Stir well and reheat. Add the salt and pepper and serve.

Quick Cream of Chicken Soup

Yield: 1 quart

2 TABLESPOONS SOFT MARGARINE
3 TABLESPOONS UNBLEACHED ALL-PURPOSE FLOUR
3 CUPS *CHICKEN BROTH* (SEE PAGE 20)
1 CUP HALF-AND-HALF
1 CUP COOKED FINELY CHOPPED CHICKEN
SALT AND FRESHLY GROUND BLACK PEPPER TO TASTE
CHOPPED FRESH CHIVES, FOR GARNISH

In a large saucepan, melt the margarine and blend in the flour. Gradually add the *Chicken Broth* and cook until thickened, stirring frequently. Add the half-and-half and chicken. Simmer for 10 minutes. Add the salt and pepper. Garnish each serving with the chives and serve.

Cream of Corn Soup

Yield: 1 quart

4 CUPS FRESH OR FROZEN WHOLE KERNEL CORN
3 CUPS WATER
1 TEASPOON SUGAR
2 TABLESPOONS SOFT MARGARINE
1 CUP HALF-AND-HALF
SALT AND FRESHLY GROUND BLACK PEPPER TO TASTE

In a large saucepan, cook the corn in the water on medium heat for 15 minutes, or until the corn is tender. Drain and reserve the cooking liquid in the saucepan.

Puree the corn in a blender or food processor, or force through a metal colander or food mill. Return the corn to the saucepan.

Add the sugar and margarine and heat to boiling. Reduce heat and add the half-and-half. Simmer for 5 minutes. Add the salt and pepper and serve.

Cream of Cucumber Soup

Yield: 1½ quarts

4 MEDIUM CUCUMBERS, PEELED AND CHOPPED

4 STALKS CELERY, CHOPPED

2 TABLESPOONS CHOPPED ONIONS

1 TABLESPOON CHOPPED GREEN BELL PEPPER

2 CUPS *CHICKEN BROTH* (SEE PAGE 20)

4 TABLESPOONS SOFT MARGARINE

4 TABLESPOONS UNBLEACHED ALL-PURPOSE FLOUR

2 CUPS LOW-FAT MILK

1 CUP HALF-AND-HALF

SALT AND FRESHLY GROUND BLACK PEPPER TO TASTE

In a large soup pot, cook the cucumbers, celery, onions, and green pepper in the *Chicken Broth* on medium heat for 20 minutes, or until the vegetables are tender. Drain and reserve the cooking liquid in the soup pot.

Puree the vegetables in a blender or food processor, or force through a metal colander or food mill. Return the vegetables to the soup pot.

In a medium-size saucepan, melt the margarine and blend in the flour. Gradually add 2 cups soup liquid and the milk and cook until thickened, stirring frequently. Add the milk mixture to the vegetable mixture. Add the half-and-half. Stir well and reheat. Add the salt and pepper and serve.

Cream of Egg Drop Soup

Yield: 1½ quarts

4 CUPS LOW-FAT MILK
3 EGGS, WELL BEATEN
SALT AND FRESHLY GROUND WHITE PEPPER TO TASTE
TOASTED BREAD CRUMBS, FOR GARNISH

In a large soup pot, scald the milk. Gradually add the eggs, stirring constantly. Add the salt and pepper.

Garnish each serving with the bread crumbs and serve.

Cream of Mushroom Soup

Yield: 1 quart

2 TABLESPOONS SOFT MARGARINE
½ POUND FRESH MUSHROOMS, FINELY CHOPPED
1 TABLESPOON UNBLEACHED ALL-PURPOSE FLOUR
1 CUP *CHICKEN BROTH* (SEE PAGE 20)
2 CUPS LOW-FAT MILK
½ CUP HALF-AND-HALF
SALT AND FRESHLY GROUND BLACK PEPPER TO TASTE

In a large saucepan, melt the margarine and sauté the mushrooms for 5 minutes. Cover and cook on medium heat for 5 minutes more.

Blend in the flour. Gradually add the *Chicken Broth* and cook until thickened, stirring frequently. Add the milk and cook on medium heat for 2 minutes. Reduce heat and add the half-and-half. Simmer for 2 minutes. Add the salt and pepper and serve.

Cream of Onion Soup

Yield: 1½ quarts

½ CUP SOFT MARGARINE
6 MEDIUM ONIONS, CHOPPED
3 CUPS *CHICKEN BROTH* (SEE PAGE 20)
4 TABLESPOONS UNBLEACHED ALL-PURPOSE FLOUR
2 CUPS LOW-FAT MILK
1 EGG YOLK, SLIGHTLY BEATEN
1 TABLESPOON CHOPPED RED BELL PEPPER
SALT AND FRESHLY GROUND BLACK PEPPER TO TASTE
GRATED PARMESAN CHEESE, FOR GARNISH

In a large soup pot, melt 6 tablespoons margarine and sauté the onions until transparent. Add the *Chicken Broth.* Simmer, covered, for 30 minutes. Drain and reserve the cooking liquid in the soup pot.

Puree the onions in a blender or food processor, or force through a metal colander or food mill. Return the onions to the soup pot.

In a medium-size saucepan, melt the remaining margarine and blend in the flour. Gradually add the milk and cook until thickened, stirring frequently. Add the egg yolk and cook on low heat for 2 minutes, stirring frequently. Add the egg mixture and bell pepper to the onion mixture. Stir well and reheat. Add the salt and pepper.

Garnish each serving with the cheese and serve.

Mock Oyster Soup

Yield: 1 quart

1½ CUPS PEELED AND CHOPPED SALSIFY
1½ CUPS WATER
1 TABLESPOON SOFT MARGARINE
3 CUPS LOW-FAT MILK
½ CUP HALF-AND-HALF
SALT AND FRESHLY GROUND WHITE PEPPER TO TASTE

In a large saucepan, cook the salsify in the water on medium heat for 30 minutes, or until the salsify is tender. Drain and reserve the cooking liquid in the saucepan.

Puree the salsify in a blender or food processor, or force through a metal colander or food mill. Return the salsify to the saucepan.

Add the margarine, milk, and half-and-half and stir well. Simmer for 10 minutes. Add the salt and pepper and serve.

Cream of Potato & Cheese Soup

Yield: 2 quarts

3 MEDIUM POTATOES, CHOPPED
1 MEDIUM ONION, CHOPPED
2 CUPS WATER
2 TABLESPOONS SOFT MARGARINE
2 TABLESPOONS UNBLEACHED ALL-PURPOSE FLOUR
4 CUPS LOW-FAT MILK
½ CUP SHREDDED LOW-FAT CHEDDAR CHEESE
SALT AND FRESHLY GROUND WHITE PEPPER TO TASTE

In a large soup pot, cook the potatoes and onion in the water on medium heat for 25 minutes, or until the vegetables are tender. Drain and reserve the cooking liquid in the soup pot.

Puree the vegetables in a blender or food processor, or force through a metal colander or food mill. Return the vegetables to the soup pot.

In a large saucepan, melt the margarine and blend in the flour. Gradually add the milk and cook until thickened, stirring frequently. Add the cheese and cook until the cheese is melted. Add the cheese mixture to the potato mixture. Stir well and reheat. Add the salt and pepper and serve.

Peanut Butter Soup

Yield: 1 quart

4 CUPS LOW-FAT MILK
1 TEASPOON ONION JUICE
1 TABLESPOON CHOPPED CELERY
1 CUP PEANUT BUTTER
2 TABLESPOONS LOW-FAT MILK
1 TABLESPOON CORNSTARCH
SALT AND FRESHLY GROUND BLACK PEPPER TO TASTE
COARSELY GROUND PEANUTS, FOR GARNISH

In the top of a double boiler, cook the 4 cups milk, onion juice, celery, and peanut butter over hot water for 10 minutes.

In a small saucepan, heat the 2 tablespoons milk and blend in the cornstarch. Cook until smooth and thickened. Add the cornstarch mixture to the peanut butter mixture.

Puree the combined mixture in a blender or food processor, or force through a metal colander or food mill. Return the mixture to the double boiler. Stir well and reheat. Add the salt and pepper.

Garnish each serving with the peanuts and serve.

Cream of Pea Soup

Yield: 1½ quarts

3 CUPS FRESH OR FROZEN PEAS
1 TEASPOON MINCED ONIONS
1 CUP WATER
3 TABLESPOONS SOFT MARGARINE
3 TABLESPOONS UNBLEACHED ALL-PURPOSE FLOUR
3 CUPS LOW-FAT MILK
½ CUP HALF-AND-HALF
SALT AND FRESHLY GROUND BLACK PEPPER TO TASTE

In a large soup pot, cook the peas and onions in the water on medium heat for 15 minutes, or until the vegetables are tender. Drain and reserve the cooking liquid in the soup pot.

Puree the vegetables in a blender or food processor, or force through a metal colander or food mill. Return the vegetables to the soup pot.

In a large saucepan, melt the margarine and blend in the flour. Gradually add the milk and cook until thickened, stirring frequently. Add the milk mixture and half-and-half to the pea mixture. Stir well and reheat. Add the salt and pepper and serve.

Cream of Spinach Soup

Yield: 1 quart

1½ CUPS FINELY CHOPPED FRESH SPINACH
4 CUPS LOW-FAT MILK
2 TABLESPOONS SOFT MARGARINE
¼ TEASPOON GRATED LEMON PEEL
1 TABLESPOON CORNSTARCH
1 TABLESPOON COLD WATER
SALT AND FRESHLY GROUND BLACK PEPPER TO TASTE

In a large saucepan, cook the spinach with the milk, margarine, and lemon peel on medium heat for 5 minutes, or until the spinach wilts and is barely cooked.

In a small bowl, blend the cornstarch with the cold water. Add the cornstarch mixture to the spinach mixture. Cook for 5 minutes or until slightly thickened. Add the salt and pepper and serve.

Cream of Tomato Soup

Yield: 1 quart

3½ CUPS CHOPPED TOMATOES
2 TEASPOONS SUGAR
2 TABLESPOONS CHOPPED ONIONS
1 CUP WATER
5 WHOLE CLOVES
5 WHOLE PEPPERCORNS
½ CUP CHOPPED FRESH PARSLEY
1 BAY LEAF
3 TABLESPOONS SOFT MARGARINE
3 TABLESPOONS UNBLEACHED ALL-PURPOSE FLOUR
3 CUPS LOW-FAT MILK
½ CUP HALF-AND-HALF
SALT AND FRESHLY GROUND BLACK PEPPER TO TASTE

In a large saucepan, combine the tomatoes, sugar, onions, and water. Tie the cloves, peppercorns, parsley, and bay leaf in a cheesecloth bag and add to the saucepan. Simmer, covered, for 25 minutes. Discard the cheesecloth bag.

Puree the tomato mixture in a blender or food processor, or force through a metal colander or food mill. Return the tomato mixture to the saucepan. Add enough water to make 2 cups, if necessary. Keep the tomato mixture hot.

In a large saucepan, melt the margarine and blend in the flour. Gradually add the milk and cook until thickened, stirring frequently. Add the half-and-half and heat to boiling.

Gradually add the boiling milk mixture to the tomato mixture, stirring frequently. Add the salt and pepper and serve.

Cream of Vegetable Soup

Yield: 1½ quarts

3 MEDIUM POTATOES, CHOPPED

2 STALKS CELERY, CHOPPED

1 MEDIUM ONION, CHOPPED

⅛ TEASPOON DRIED SAGE

1 BAY LEAF

2 CUPS CHOPPED ASPARAGUS

4 CUPS WATER

2 TABLESPOONS SOFT MARGARINE

2 TABLESPOONS UNBLEACHED ALL-PURPOSE FLOUR

2 CUPS LOW-FAT MILK

SALT AND FRESHLY GROUND BLACK PEPPER TO TASTE

In a large soup pot, cook the potatoes, celery, onion, sage, bay leaf, and asparagus in the water on medium heat for 25 minutes, or until the vegetables are tender. Drain and reserve the cooking liquid in the soup pot. Remove the bay leaf and discard.

Puree the vegetables in a blender or food processor, or force through a metal colander or food mill. Return the vegetables to the soup pot.

In a medium-size saucepan, melt the margarine and blend in the flour. Gradually add the milk and cook until thickened, stirring frequently. Add the milk mixture to the vegetable mixture. Stir well and reheat. Add the salt and pepper and serve.

Vinegar Soup

Yield: 2½ quarts

2 CUPS SLICED POTATOES
2 QUARTS WATER
4 TABLESPOONS SOFT MARGARINE
3 TABLESPOONS UNBLEACHED ALL-PURPOSE FLOUR
2 CUPS HALF-AND-HALF
SALT AND FRESHLY GROUND WHITE PEPPER TO TASTE
½ CUP WHITE WINE VINEGAR

In a large soup pot, cook the potatoes in the water on medium heat for 25 minutes, or until the potatoes are tender.

In a small saucepan, melt the margarine and blend in the flour. Gradually add 1 cup soup liquid and cook until thickened, stirring frequently. Add the soup liquid mixture to the potato mixture. In a medium-size saucepan, scald the half-and-half and add to the potato mixture. Add the salt and pepper.

Before serving, add the vinegar and stir well. Serve.

Bisques

Bisques are not suitable for freezing.

Lobster Bisque

Yield: 1½ quarts

2 CUPS COOKED CHOPPED LOBSTER MEAT
2 CUPS COLD WATER
4 TABLESPOONS SOFT MARGARINE
3 TABLESPOONS UNBLEACHED ALL-PURPOSE FLOUR
4 CUPS LOW-FAT MILK
SALT AND FRESHLY GROUND BLACK PEPPER TO TASTE
DASH CAYENNE PEPPER

In a large soup pot, combine the lobster meat and the cold water. Simmer, covered, for 15 minutes.

In a large saucepan, melt the margarine and blend in the flour. Gradually add the milk and cook until thickened, stirring frequently. Add the milk mixture to the lobster mixture. Stir well and reheat. Add the salt, pepper, and cayenne pepper and serve.

Crab Bisque

Yield: 1 quart

3 TABLESPOONS SOFT MARGARINE
1 MEDIUM ONION, SLICED
4 TABLESPOONS UNBLEACHED ALL-PURPOSE FLOUR
3 CUPS LOW-FAT MILK
1 CUP *CHICKEN BROTH* (SEE PAGE 20)
1½ CUPS COOKED CRABMEAT
¼ CUP CHOPPED FRESH PARSLEY
½ CUP HALF-AND-HALF
SALT AND FRESHLY GROUND BLACK PEPPER TO TASTE

In a large saucepan, melt the margarine and sauté the onion until transparent and golden brown. Blend in the flour. Gradually add the milk and *Chicken Broth* and cook until thickened, stirring frequently. Add the crabmeat and parsley and cook on low heat for 10 minutes.

Puree the crabmeat mixture in a blender or food processor, or force through a metal colander or food mill. Return the crabmeat mixture to the saucepan.

Add the half-and-half. Stir well and reheat. Add the salt and pepper and serve.

Shrimp Bisque

Yield: 1 quart

3 TABLESPOONS SOFT MARGARINE
2 CUPS PEELED, DEVEINED, AND CHOPPED SHRIMP
2 TABLESPOONS CHOPPED ONIONS
1 SMALL CARROT, CHOPPED
1 STALK CELERY, CHOPPED
½ CUP SLICED FRESH MUSHROOMS
3 CUPS *WHITE STOCK* (SEE PAGE 12)
SALT AND FRESHLY GROUND BLACK PEPPER TO TASTE
DASH CAYENNE PEPPER
1 CUP WHITE WINE

In a large saucepan, melt the margarine and add the shrimp, onions, carrot, celery, mushrooms, and *White Stock*. Simmer, covered, for 20 minutes.

Puree the shrimp mixture in a blender or food processor, or force through a metal colander or food mill. Return the shrimp mixture to the saucepan. Reheat. Add the salt and pepper.

Before serving, add the wine and stir well. Serve.

Oyster Bisque

Yield: 1 quart

Two 8-ounce containers fresh oysters
2 tablespoons soft margarine
2 tablespoons unbleached all-purpose flour
3 cups low-fat milk
½ teaspoon ground paprika
⅛ teaspoon ground nutmeg
2 egg yolks, well beaten
¼ cup half-and-half
Salt and freshly ground black pepper to taste
Finely chopped cilantro, for garnish

In a colander, thoroughly rinse the oysters with cold water and cut in half with scissors. Set aside.

In a large saucepan, melt the margarine and blend in the flour. Gradually add the milk and cook until thickened, stirring frequently. Add the paprika, nutmeg, and reserved oysters. Keep the oyster mixture warm on the *lowest* heat.

In a small bowl, beat together the egg yolks and half-and-half until thick. Add ¼ cup soup liquid, one tablespoon at a time, to the egg mixture. Blend well. Add the egg mixture to the oyster mixture. Stir well and reheat. Add the salt and pepper.

Garnish each serving with the cilantro and serve.

Clam Bisque

Yield: 2 quarts

If fresh clams are not available, substitute one 10-ounce can of whole or chopped clams with liquid for the fresh clams.

12 FRESH CLAMS IN THE SHELL
2 CUPS WATER
2 CUPS *CHICKEN BROTH* (SEE PAGE 20)
3 TABLESPOONS SOFT MARGARINE
2 TABLESPOONS CHOPPED ONIONS
4 TABLESPOONS UNBLEACHED ALL-PURPOSE FLOUR
1 BAY LEAF
2 CUPS HEATED HALF-AND-HALF
1 TEASPOON WORCESTERSHIRE SAUCE
SALT AND FRESHLY GROUND BLACK PEPPER TO TASTE

Clean the clam shells thoroughly with a vegetable brush. In a large soup pot, cover the unopened clams with the water. Bring to a boil. Reduce heat and simmer, covered, for 5 minutes, or until the shells are opened.

As each shell opens, remove the clams and set aside. Pour the liquor from each shell into a small bowl and set aside.

Remove the thin skin from the reserved clams and cut off the black end and discard. Chop the tough parts of the clams and leave the soft parts whole. Set aside.

Add the *Chicken Broth* to the soup pot and simmer for 20 minutes. In a large saucepan, melt the margarine and sauté the onions until transparent. Blend in the flour. Gradually add the reserved clam liquor and cook until thickened, stirring frequently. Add the bay leaf and the reserved clams and cook on low heat for 5 minutes. Remove the bay leaf and discard.

Add the onion and clam mixture, half-and-half, and Worcestershire sauce to the soup pot. Stir well and reheat. Add the salt and pepper and serve.

Chicken Bisque

Yield: 1 quart

2 TABLESPOONS SOFT MARGARINE
1½ TABLESPOONS UNBLEACHED ALL-PURPOSE FLOUR
3 CUPS *CHICKEN BROTH* (SEE PAGE 20)
1 CUP COOKED FINELY CHOPPED CHICKEN
1 CUP LOW-FAT MILK
SALT AND FRESHLY GROUND BLACK PEPPER TO TASTE
CHOPPED FRESH WATERCRESS, FOR GARNISH

In a large saucepan, melt the margarine and blend in the flour. Gradually add the *Chicken Broth* and chicken and cook until thickened, stirring frequently.

In a small saucepan, scald the milk. Add the scalded milk to the large saucepan and stir well. Add the salt and pepper.

Garnish each serving with the watercress and serve.

Tomato Bisque

Yield: 1½ quarts

2½ CUPS CHOPPED TOMATOES
1 TEASPOON SUGAR
½ CUP WATER
3 TABLESPOONS SOFT MARGARINE
1 SMALL ONION, CHOPPED
1 BAY LEAF
¼ CUP CHOPPED FRESH PARSLEY
1 CUP DRY BREAD CRUMBS
4 CUPS LOW-FAT MILK
SALT AND FRESHLY GROUND BLACK PEPPER TO TASTE

In a large soup pot, cook the tomatoes and sugar in the water on medium heat for 20 minutes, or until the tomatoes are tender.

In a small saucepan, melt the margarine and sauté the onion until transparent. Add the onion mixture, bay leaf, and parsley to the soup pot and cook for 5 minutes. Remove the bay leaf and discard.

Puree the tomato and onion mixture in a blender or food processor, or force through a metal colander or food mill. Return the mixture to the soup pot.

In a large saucepan, combine the bread crumbs and the milk and heat to scalding. Add the milk mixture to the soup pot and stir well. Add the salt and pepper and serve.

Fish & Shellfish Soups

Bouillabaisse

Yield: 2½ quarts

Vary the types and amounts of fish and shellfish in this recipe according to preference and availability.

24 FRESH CLAMS, MUSSELS, OR OYSTERS IN THE SHELL
2 CUPS BOILING WATER
2 POUNDS HADDOCK OR PERCH, SKINNED, CLEANED, AND CUT
    INTO FILLETS
4 CUPS BOILING WATER
½ CUP VEGETABLE OIL
2 CUPS PEELED AND DEVEINED SHRIMP
1 CUP COOKED LOBSTER MEAT
1 CUP COOKED CRABMEAT
6 MEDIUM TOMATOES, CHOPPED
2 TABLESPOONS FINELY CHOPPED ONIONS
2 TABLESPOONS FINELY CHOPPED CELERY
2 CLOVES GARLIC, MINCED
1 TEASPOON GROUND SAGE
1 TEASPOON GROUND THYME
1 TEASPOON WHOLE SAFFRON
2 BAY LEAVES
1 TEASPOON GROUND PAPRIKA
DASH CAYENNE PEPPER
½ CUP DRY SHERRY
SALT AND FRESHLY GROUND BLACK PEPPER TO TASTE
LEMON SLICES, FOR GARNISH
CHOPPED FRESH PARSLEY, FOR GARNISH

Clean the shellfish thoroughly with a vegetable brush. In a large soup pot, cover the unopened shellfish with the 2 cups boiling water. As each shell opens, remove the meat and set aside. Pour the liquor from each shell into the soup pot.

Add the fish and the 4 cups boiling water to the soup pot. Simmer, covered, for 10 minutes. Drain. Reserve the soup stock and set aside the meat.

In the same soup pot, heat the oil and add all the reserved meat and all the remaining ingredients, except the sherry, salt, pepper, lemon, and parsley. Simmer for 10 minutes, stirring frequently.

Add the reserved soup stock and sherry and cook on very low heat for 30 minutes. Remove the bay leaves and discard. Add the salt and pepper.

Garnish each serving with a lemon slice and the parsley and serve.

Clam Soup

Yield: 1½ quarts

If fresh clams are not available, substitute three 6½-ounce cans of whole or chopped clams with liquid for the fresh clams.

24 FRESH CLAMS IN THE SHELL
4 CUPS BOILING WATER
2 CUPS WATER
DASH CAYENNE PEPPER
4 CUPS LOW-FAT MILK
2 TABLESPOONS SOFT MARGARINE
SALT AND FRESHLY GROUND BLACK PEPPER TO TASTE

Clean the clams thoroughly with a vegetable brush. In a large soup pot, cover the unopened clams with the 4 cups boiling water. As each shell opens, remove the clams and set aside. Pour the liquor from each shell into the soup pot.

Add the 2 cups water, cayenne pepper, and reserved clams to the soup pot. Simmer, covered, for 30 minutes. Add the milk and margarine and simmer for 5 minutes more. Add the salt and pepper and serve. **Note:** This soup should not be frozen.

Lobster Soup

Yield: 2 quarts

4 CUPS COOKED CHOPPED LOBSTER MEAT
2 ANCHOVIES OR SMOKED FISH FILLETS
4 CUPS WATER
1 SMALL ONION, CHOPPED
¼ TEASPOON DRIED THYME
½ TEASPOON DRIED MARJORAM
¼ CUP CHOPPED FRESH PARSLEY
1 STRIP LEMON PEEL
⅛ TEASPOON GROUND NUTMEG
2 TABLESPOONS SOFT MARGARINE
1 TABLESPOON UNBLEACHED ALL-PURPOSE FLOUR
2 CUPS LOW-FAT MILK
2 CUPS HALF-AND-HALF
SALT AND FRESHLY GROUND BLACK PEPPER TO TASTE

In a large soup pot, cover the lobster meat and anchovies with the water. Tie the onion, thyme, marjoram, parsley, and lemon peel in a cheesecloth bag and add to the soup pot. Simmer, covered, for 30 minutes. Discard the cheesecloth bag.

In a medium-size saucepan, melt the margarine and blend in the flour. Gradually add the milk and cook until slightly thickened, stirring frequently. Slowly add the milk mixture and half-and-half to the soup pot. Stir well and reheat. Add the salt and pepper and serve. **Note:** This soup should not be frozen.

Crab Soup

Yield: 1 quart

1 CUP COOKED FLAKED CRABMEAT
2 HARD-COOKED EGGS, CHOPPED
3 CUPS HALF-AND-HALF
⅛ TEASPOON GROUND MUSTARD
⅛ TEASPOON GROUND MACE
4 TEASPOONS SOFT MARGARINE
SALT AND FRESHLY GROUND BLACK PEPPER TO TASTE
LEMON SLICES, FOR GARNISH
CHOPPED FRESH PARSLEY, FOR GARNISH

In a double boiler, cook the crabmeat, eggs, half-and-half, mustard, and mace over boiling water for 10 minutes, or until quite hot, but not boiling. Add the margarine and stir well. Add the salt and pepper.

Garnish each serving with a lemon slice and the parsley and serve. **Note:** This soup should not be frozen.

Salmon Soup

Yield: 2½ quarts

4 TABLESPOONS SOFT MARGARINE
2 QUARTS LOW-FAT MILK
2 CUPS COOKED FLAKED RED OR PINK SALMON
SALT AND FRESHLY GROUND WHITE PEPPER TO TASTE

In a large soup pot, melt the margarine and brown lightly. Add the milk and salmon. Simmer, covered, for 10 minutes. Add the salt and pepper and serve. **Note:** This soup should not be frozen.

Catfish Soup

Yield: 2½ quarts

6 SMALL CATFISH, SKINNED, CLEANED, AND CUT INTO FILLETS
1½ POUNDS COOKED LEAN HAM, CUT INTO 1-INCH CUBES
¼ CUP CHOPPED FRESH PARSLEY
1 TEASPOON DRIED MARJORAM
3 STALKS CELERY, COARSELY CHOPPED
2 QUARTS COLD WATER
4 TABLESPOONS SOFT MARGARINE
4 TABLESPOONS UNBLEACHED ALL-PURPOSE FLOUR
4 CUPS LOW-FAT MILK
2 EGG YOLKS, SLIGHTLY BEATEN
SALT AND FRESHLY GROUND BLACK PEPPER TO TASTE

In a large soup pot, cover the catfish, ham, parsley, marjoram, and celery with the cold water. Simmer, covered, for 30 minutes, or until the fish is tender, but not overcooked.

Strain the soup stock through three thicknesses of cheesecloth and return the stock to the soup pot. Return the fish and ham to the soup pot. Discard the cooked herbs and celery. Reheat the stock.

In a large saucepan, melt the margarine and blend in the flour. Gradually add the milk and cook until thickened, stirring frequently. Add the egg yolks and cook on low heat for 2 minutes. Add the egg mixture to the fish and ham mixture. Stir well and reheat. Add the salt and pepper and serve. **Note:** This soup should not be frozen.

Green Turtle Soup

Yield: 2 quarts

Green turtle meat is usually available in specialty sections in large supermarkets. Any cooked or canned turtle meat may be substituted for the green turtle meat in this recipe.

2 CUPS GREEN TURTLE MEAT, CUT INTO ½ -INCH CUBES
6 CUPS *BROWN STOCK* (SEE PAGE 11)
4 WHOLE CLOVES
4 WHOLE PEPPERCORNS
1 BAY LEAF
½ TEASPOON GROUND MACE
¼ TEASPOON DRIED SAVORY
½ TEASPOON DRIED MARJORAM
¼ TEASPOON DRIED THYME
¼ TEASPOON DRIED SAGE
3 TABLESPOONS SOFT MARGARINE
1 SMALL ONION, CHOPPED
3 TABLESPOONS UNBLEACHED ALL-PURPOSE FLOUR
SALT TO TASTE
DASH CAYENNE PEPPER
¼ CUP DRY SHERRY
LEMON SLICES, FOR GARNISH

In a large soup pot, cover the turtle meat with 4 cups *Brown Stock.* Tie the cloves, peppercorns, bay leaf, mace, savory, marjoram, thyme, and sage in a cheesecloth bag and add to the soup pot. Simmer, covered, for 30 minutes. Discard the cheesecloth bag.

In a medium-size saucepan, melt the margarine and sauté the onion until transparent. Blend in the flour. Gradually add the remaining *Brown Stock* and cook until thickened, stirring frequently. Add the stock mixture to the turtle mixture. Stir well and reheat. Add the salt, cayenne pepper, and sherry.

Garnish each serving with a lemon slice and serve.

Turtle Soup

Yield: 2½ quarts

2 QUARTS *CHICKEN BROTH* (SEE PAGE 20)

¼ TEASPOON DRIED THYME

1 BAY LEAF

¼ CUP CHOPPED FRESH PARSLEY

1½ POUNDS COOKED OR CANNED TURTLE MEAT, CUT INTO ½-INCH CUBES

½ POUND FRESH MUSHROOMS, SLICED

1 TABLESPOON CORNSTARCH

1 TABLESPOON COLD WATER

SALT AND FRESHLY GROUND BLACK PEPPER TO TASTE

HARD-COOKED EGGS, SLICED

LEMON SLICES, FOR GARNISH

In a large soup pot, add the *Chicken Broth*. Tie the thyme, bay leaf, and parsley in a cheesecloth bag and add to the soup pot. Simmer, covered, for 15 minutes. Discard the cheesecloth bag.

Add the turtle meat and mushrooms. Simmer for 5 minutes. In a small bowl, combine the cornstarch and the cold water and stir to a thin paste. Add the cornstarch mixture to the turtle mixture and cook until slightly thickened, stirring frequently. Add the salt and pepper. Put two egg slices into each bowl and pour the soup over the egg slices.

Garnish each serving with a lemon slice and serve.

Chowders

Chowders are not suitable for freezing.

New England Clam Chowder

Yield: 3 quarts

If fresh clams are not available, substitute three 6½-ounce cans of whole or chopped clams with liquid for the fresh clams.

24 FRESH CLAMS IN THE SHELL
4 CUPS BOILING WATER
1 TABLESPOON SOFT MARGARINE
1 SMALL ONION, CHOPPED
2 SLICES LEAN BACON, COOKED AND CRUMBLED
4 MEDIUM POTATOES, THINLY SLICED
4 CUPS WATER
1 QUART LOW-FAT MILK OR HALF-AND-HALF
1 TABLESPOON SOFT MARGARINE
SALT AND FRESHLY GROUND BLACK PEPPER TO TASTE

Clean the clams thoroughly with a vegetable brush. In a large soup pot, cover the unopened clams with the 4 cups boiling water. As each shell opens, remove the clams and set aside. Pour the liquor from each shell into the soup pot.

Remove the thin skin from the reserved clams and cut off the black end and discard. Chop the tough parts of the clams and leave the soft parts whole. Set aside.

In a small saucepan, melt the margarine and sauté the onion until transparent. Add the onion mixture, bacon, potatoes, and the 4 cups water to the soup pot. Simmer, covered, for 25 minutes, or until the potatoes are tender.

Add the reserved clams, milk, and margarine and simmer for 10 minutes. Add the salt and pepper and serve.

Manhattan Clam Chowder

Yield: 2 quarts

If fresh clams are not available, substitute three 6½-ounce cans of whole or chopped clams with liquid for the fresh clams.

24 FRESH CLAMS IN THE SHELL
4 CUPS BOILING WATER
1 TABLESPOON VEGETABLE OIL
1 SMALL ONION, SLICED
1 CLOVE GARLIC, MINCED
¼ POUND LEAN BACON, COOKED AND CRUMBLED
¼ CUP CHOPPED CELERY
¼ CUP CHOPPED CARROTS
1 CUP CHOPPED POTATOES
3 CUPS WATER
2 CUPS COOKED CHOPPED TOMATOES
⅛ TEASPOON DRIED THYME
SALT AND FRESHLY GROUND BLACK PEPPER TO TASTE

Clean the clams thoroughly with a vegetable brush. In a large soup pot, cover the unopened clams with the 4 cups boiling water. As each shell opens, remove the clams and set aside. Pour the liquor from each shell into the soup pot.

Remove the thin skin from the reserved clams and cut off the black end and discard. Chop the tough parts of the clams and leave the soft parts whole. Set aside.

In a small saucepan, heat the oil and sauté the onion and garlic until the onion is transparent. Add the onion mixture, bacon, celery, carrots, potatoes, 3 cups water, tomatoes, and thyme to the soup pot. Simmer, covered, for 25 minutes, or until the vegetables are tender.

Add the reserved clams and simmer for 10 minutes. Add the salt and pepper and serve.

Crab Chowder

Yield: 1½ quarts

4 TABLESPOONS SOFT MARGARINE
1 SMALL ONION, CHOPPED
2 TABLESPOONS UNBLEACHED ALL-PURPOSE FLOUR
4 CUPS LOW-FAT MILK
2 CUPS COOKED FLAKED CRABMEAT
1 CUP HALF-AND-HALF
SALT AND FRESHLY GROUND WHITE PEPPER TO TASTE
DASH CAYENNE PEPPER

In a large soup pot, melt the margarine and sauté the onion until transparent. Blend in the flour. Gradually add the milk and cook until thickened, stirring frequently. Add the crabmeat and half-and-half. Stir well and reheat. Add the salt, pepper, and cayenne pepper and serve.

Lobster Chowder

Yield: 2 quarts

1 TABLESPOON VEGETABLE OIL
1 SMALL ONION, CHOPPED
2 TABLESPOONS UNBLEACHED ALL-PURPOSE FLOUR
¼ POUND LEAN BACON, COOKED AND CRUMBLED
4 CUPS LOW-FAT MILK
2 CUPS COOKED CHOPPED LOBSTER MEAT
3 TABLESPOONS SOFT MARGARINE
1½ CUPS HALF-AND-HALF
SALT AND FRESHLY GROUND BLACK PEPPER TO TASTE
DASH CAYENNE PEPPER

In a large soup pot, heat the oil and sauté the onion until transparent. Blend in the flour and bacon. Gradually add the milk and cook until thickened, stirring frequently. Add the lobster meat and simmer for 10 minutes.

Add the margarine and half-and-half. Stir well and reheat. Add the salt, pepper, and cayenne pepper and serve.

Shrimp Chowder

Yield: 2 quarts

2 CUPS CHOPPED POTATOES
1 SMALL ONION, CHOPPED
2 CUPS WATER
4 TABLESPOONS SOFT MARGARINE
2 TABLESPOONS UNBLEACHED ALL-PURPOSE FLOUR
4 CUPS LOW-FAT MILK
2 CUPS COOKED CHOPPED SHRIMP
1 CUP HALF-AND-HALF
SALT AND FRESHLY GROUND BLACK PEPPER TO TASTE

In a large soup pot, cover the potatoes and onion with the water. Simmer, covered, for 25 minutes, or until the vegetables are tender.

In a large saucepan, melt the margarine and blend in the flour. Gradually add the milk and cook until thickened, stirring frequently. Add the milk mixture and shrimp to the soup pot. Simmer for 5 minutes.

Add the half-and-half. Stir well and reheat. Add the salt and pepper and serve.

Oyster Chowder

Yield: 2 quarts

TWO 8-OUNCE CONTAINERS FRESH OYSTERS
2 TABLESPOONS VEGETABLE OIL
2 SMALL ONIONS, CHOPPED
¼ POUND LEAN BACON, COOKED AND CRUMBLED
2 CUPS CHOPPED POTATOES
2 CUPS WATER
1 TABLESPOON SOFT MARGARINE
1 TABLESPOON UNBLEACHED ALL-PURPOSE FLOUR
4 CUPS LOW-FAT MILK
SALT AND FRESHLY GROUND BLACK PEPPER TO TASTE

In a colander, thoroughly rinse the oysters with cold water. Set aside.

In a large soup pot, heat the oil and sauté the onions until transparent. Add the bacon, potatoes, and water. Simmer, covered, for 25 minutes, or until the potatoes are tender.

In a large saucepan, melt the margarine and blend in the flour. Gradually add the milk and cook until thickened, stirring frequently. Add the milk mixture and the reserved oysters to the soup pot. Simmer, covered, for 25 minutes. Add the salt and pepper and serve.

Coney Island Chowder

Yield: 3 quarts

3 POUNDS FRESH FISH (PERCH, HADDOCK, COD, OR CATFISH),
    SKINNED, CLEANED, AND CUT INTO FILLETS
1 TABLESPOON VEGETABLE OIL
1 SMALL ONION, CHOPPED
2 QUARTS *FISH STOCK* (SEE PAGE 13)
½ TEASPOON DRIED THYME
½ TEASPOON DRIED SAVORY
6 WHOLE CLOVES
1 BAY LEAF
¼ CUP CHOPPED FRESH PARSLEY
¼ POUND LEAN BACON, COOKED AND CRUMBLED
4 MEDIUM POTATOES, SLICED
3 CUPS TOMATO JUICE OR PUREE
3 TABLESPOONS SOFT MARGARINE
3 TABLESPOONS UNBLEACHED ALL-PURPOSE FLOUR
SALT AND FRESHLY GROUND BLACK PEPPER TO TASTE

Cut the fish into 2-inch pieces and set aside.

In a large soup pot, heat the oil and sauté the onion until transparent. Add the *Fish Stock.* Tie the thyme, savory, cloves, bay leaf, and parsley in a cheesecloth bag and add to the soup pot. Add the reserved fish, bacon, potatoes, and tomato juice. Simmer, covered, for 25 minutes, or until the potatoes are tender and the fish is cooked. Discard the cheesecloth bag.

In a small saucepan, melt the margarine and blend in the flour. Gradually add 1 cup soup liquid and cook until thickened, stirring frequently. Add the soup liquid mixture to the soup pot. Stir well and reheat. Add the salt and pepper and serve.

Fish Chowder

Yield: 1 quart

1 TABLESPOON VEGETABLE OIL
1 SMALL ONION, CHOPPED
1 MEDIUM POTATO, CHOPPED
1 CUP CHOPPED TOMATOES
2 CUPS *BEEF BROTH* (SEE PAGE 21)
1 TABLESPOON SOFT MARGARINE
2 CUPS COOKED FLAKED SALMON OR OTHER COOKED FISH
SALT AND FRESHLY GROUND BLACK PEPPER TO TASTE

In a large saucepan, heat the oil and sauté the onion until transparent. Add the potato, tomatoes, *Beef Broth,* and margarine. Simmer, covered, for 20 minutes, or until the vegetables are tender.

Add the salmon and simmer for 5 minutes. Add the salt and pepper and serve.

Chicken Chowder

Yield: 2 quarts

3 TABLESPOONS SOFT MARGARINE
1 TABLESPOON CHOPPED ONIONS
1 QUART *CHICKEN BROTH* (SEE PAGE 20)
1 QUART LOW-FAT MILK
1 CUP COOKED FINELY CHOPPED CHICKEN
2 CUPS COOKED CHOPPED POTATOES
2 TABLESPOONS UNBLEACHED ALL-PURPOSE FLOUR
SALT AND FRESHLY GROUND BLACK PEPPER TO TASTE

In a large soup pot, melt 1 tablespoon margarine and sauté the onions until transparent. Add the *Chicken Broth,* milk, chicken, and potatoes. Simmer, covered, for 10 minutes.

In a small saucepan, melt the remaining margarine and blend in the flour. Gradually add 1 cup soup liquid and cook until thickened, stirring frequently. Add the soup liquid mixture to the soup pot. Stir well and reheat. Add the salt and pepper and serve.

Corn Chowder

Yield: 2½ quarts

4 CUPS FRESH OR FROZEN WHOLE KERNEL CORN
3 CUPS WATER
2 TABLESPOONS VEGETABLE OIL
1 MEDIUM ONION, CHOPPED
¼ POUND LEAN BACON, COOKED AND CRUMBLED
4 CUPS SLICED POTATOES
2 CUPS WATER
1 CUP LOW-FAT MILK
1 CUP HALF-AND-HALF
2 TABLESPOONS SOFT MARGARINE
SALT AND FRESHLY GROUND BLACK PEPPER TO TASTE

In a large soup pot, cook the corn with the 3 cups water on medium heat for 15 minutes, or until the corn is tender.

In a small saucepan, heat the oil and sauté the onion until transparent. Add the onion mixture, bacon, potatoes, and the 2 cups water to the soup pot. Simmer, covered, for 25 minutes, or until the potatoes are tender.

Add the milk, half-and-half, and margarine and simmer for 5 minutes. Add the salt and pepper and serve.

Corn & Cheese Chowder

Yield: 1½ quarts

2 TABLESPOONS SOFT MARGARINE
1 MEDIUM ONION, CHOPPED
½ CUP CHOPPED CELERY
2 CUPS CHOPPED POTATOES
2 CUPS WATER
1 BAY LEAF
½ TEASPOON GROUND BASIL
2 CUPS CANNED CREAM-STYLE CORN
1½ CUPS LOW-FAT MILK
1 CUP COOKED CHOPPED TOMATOES
½ CUP GRATED LOW-FAT CHEDDAR CHEESE
SALT AND FRESHLY GROUND BLACK PEPPER TO TASTE
CHOPPED FRESH PARSLEY, FOR GARNISH

In a large soup pot, melt the margarine and sauté the onion and celery until the onion is transparent. Add the potatoes and water. Tie the bay leaf and basil in a cheesecloth bag and add to the soup pot. Simmer, covered, for 25 minutes, or until the potatoes are tender. Discard the cheesecloth bag.

Add the corn, milk, tomatoes, and cheese and cook on medium heat until the cheese is melted, stirring frequently. Add the salt and pepper.

Garnish each serving with the parsley and serve.

Celery Chowder

Yield: 2 quarts

1 TABLESPOON SOFT MARGARINE
1 SMALL ONION, CHOPPED
3 CUPS CHOPPED CELERY
1 CUP CHOPPED POTATOES
2 CUPS WATER
4 CUPS LOW-FAT MILK
2 HARD-COOKED EGGS, CHOPPED
SALT AND FRESHLY GROUND BLACK PEPPER TO TASTE

In a large soup pot, melt the margarine and sauté the onion until transparent. Add the celery, potatoes, and water. Simmer, covered, for 25 mintues, or until the potatoes are tender.

Add the milk and eggs. Stir well and reheat. Add the salt and pepper and serve.

Onion Chowder

Yield: 3½ quarts

3 TABLESPOONS SOFT MARGARINE
2 CUPS CHOPPED ONIONS
4 CUPS DICED POTATOES
3 QUARTS BOILING WATER
SALT AND FRESHLY GROUND WHITE PEPPER TO TASTE
CHOPPED FRESH THYME, FOR GARNISH
CHOPPED FRESH PARSLEY, FOR GARNISH

In a large soup pot, melt the margarine and sauté the onions until transparent. Add the potatoes and boiling water. Simmer, covered, for 25 minutes, or until the potatoes are tender. Add the salt and pepper.

Garnish each serving with the thyme and parsley and serve.

Vegetable Chowder

Yield: 2 quarts

2 CUPS FRESH OR FROZEN WHOLE KERNEL CORN

2 CUPS CHOPPED CELERY

1 SMALL GREEN BELL PEPPER, CORED, SEEDED, AND THINLY
   SLICED

1 MEDIUM ONION, THINLY SLICED

1 CUP COOKED CHOPPED TOMATOES

2½ CUPS WATER

4 TABLESPOONS SOFT MARGARINE

3 TABLESPOONS UNBLEACHED ALL-PURPOSE FLOUR

2 CUPS LOW-FAT MILK

SALT AND FRESHLY GROUND BLACK PEPPER TO TASTE

CHOPPED PIMIENTO, FOR GARNISH

In a large soup pot, add the corn, celery, green pepper,
onion, tomatoes, and water. Simmer, covered, for 30 minutes,
or until the vegetables are tender.

In a medium-size saucepan, melt the margarine and blend
in the flour. Gradually add the milk and cook until thickened,
stirring frequently. Add the milk mixture to the soup pot. Stir
well and reheat. Add the salt and pepper.

Garnish each serving with the pimiento and serve.

Gumbos

For these gumbo variations, fresh,
frozen, or canned okra may be used.

Crab Gumbo

Yield: 3 quarts

½ CUP SOFT MARGARINE
4 CUPS COOKED CHOPPED CRABMEAT
¼ CUP CHOPPED ONIONS
1 CLOVE GARLIC, MINCED
1 QUART OKRA, CUT INTO ½-INCH SLICES
2 QUARTS WATER
1 TABLESPOON CHOPPED RED BELL PEPPER
1 BAY LEAF
⅛ CUP CHOPPED FRESH THYME
4 TABLESPOONS SOFT MARGARINE
4 TABLESPOONS UNBLEACHED ALL-PURPOSE FLOUR
1 CUP HALF-AND-HALF
SALT AND FRESHLY GROUND BLACK PEPPER TO TASTE
COOKED WHITE RICE, FOR GARNISH

In a large skillet, melt the ½ cup margarine and sauté the crabmeat until golden brown. Remove the crabmeat and place in a large soup pot.

In the same skillet, sauté the onions, garlic, and okra until golden brown. Add the onion mixture, water, and bell pepper to the soup pot. Tie the bay leaf and thyme in a cheesecloth bag and add to the soup pot. Simmer, covered, for 45 minutes. Discard the cheesecloth bag.

In a small saucepan, melt the 4 tablespoons margarine and blend in the flour. Gradually add 1 cup soup liquid and cook until thickened, stirring frequently. Add the soup liquid mixture and half-and-half to the soup pot. Stir well and reheat. Add the salt and pepper.

Garnish each serving with the rice and serve. **Note:** This soup should not be frozen.

Chicken Gumbo

Yield: 3 quarts

¼ CUP VEGETABLE OIL
ONE 4–5-POUND STEWING CHICKEN, CUT UP
¾ POUND LEAN VEAL, CUT INTO 1½-INCH CUBES
1 SMALL ONION, SLICED
7 CUPS BOILING WATER
1 CUP FRESH OR FROZEN WHOLE KERNEL CORN
1 QUART OKRA, CUT INTO ½-INCH SLICES
SALT AND FRESHLY GROUND BLACK PEPPER TO TASTE
½ TEASPOON FILÉ POWDER OR 1 BAY LEAF, CRUSHED

In a large skillet, heat the oil and brown the chicken and veal. Add the onions. Simmer, covered, for 10 minutes, stirring occasionally. Drain off the fat.

Place the meat and onions in a large soup pot. Add the boiling water. Simmer, covered, for 2 hours. Remove the skin and bones from the chicken and discard. Return the chicken to the soup pot.

Add the corn and okra and cook on medium heat for 15 minutes. Add the salt and pepper.

Before serving, add the filé powder and stir well. Serve.

Chicken & Oyster Gumbo

Yield: 3½ quarts

¼ CUP VEGETABLE OIL

ONE 4–5-POUND STEWING CHICKEN, CUT UP

1 TABLESPOON SOFT MARGARINE

¼ CUP CHOPPED ONIONS

1 TABLESPOON CHOPPED RED BELL PEPPER

4 QUARTS WATER

FOUR 8-OUNCE CONTAINERS FRESH OYSTERS

1 QUART OKRA, CUT INTO ½-INCH SLICES

2 TABLESPOONS SOFT MARGARINE

2 TABLESPOONS UNBLEACHED ALL-PURPOSE FLOUR

SALT AND FRESHLY GROUND BLACK PEPPER TO TASTE

COOKED WHITE RICE, FOR GARNISH

In a large skillet, heat the oil and brown the chicken. Drain off the fat. Remove the chicken and place in a large soup pot.

In a small skillet, melt the 1 tablespoon margarine and sauté the onions and bell pepper. Add the onion mixture and water to the soup pot. Simmer, covered, for 2 hours.

Remove the skin and bones from the chicken and discard. Return the chicken to the soup pot. In a colander, thoroughly rinse the oysters in cold water. Add the oysters and okra to the soup pot and cook on medium heat for 15 minutes.

In a medium-size saucepan, melt the 2 tablespoons margarine and blend in the flour. Gradually add 2 cups soup liquid and cook until thickened, stirring frequently. Add the soup liquid mixture to the soup pot. Stir well and reheat. Add the salt and pepper.

Garnish each serving with the rice and serve.

Beef Gumbo

Yield: 3½ quarts

¼ CUP VEGETABLE OIL
2 POUNDS LEAN BEEF, CUT INTO 1½-INCH CUBES
½ POUND LEAN PORK, CUT INTO 1½-INCH CUBES
4 CUPS SLICED TOMATOES
3 QUARTS HOT WATER
2 QUARTS OKRA, CUT INTO ½-INCH SLICES
SALT AND FRESHLY GROUND BLACK PEPPER TO TASTE

In a large skillet, heat the oil and brown the beef and pork. Reduce heat and cook, covered, on low heat for 25 minutes, stirring occasionally. Drain off the fat.

Remove the beef and pork and place in a large soup pot. Add the tomatoes and hot water. Simmer, covered, for 1½– 2 hours.

Add the okra and cook on medium heat for 15 minutes. Add the salt and pepper and serve.

Ham Gumbo

Yield: 2½ quarts

½ CUP SOFT MARGARINE
1 SMALL ONION, CHOPPED
1 SMALL HOT RED CHILI PEPPER, SEEDED AND CHOPPED
1½ QUARTS OKRA, CUT INTO ½-INCH SLICES
2 QUARTS *CHICKEN BROTH* (SEE PAGE 20)
1 POUND COOKED HAM, CUT INTO 1½-INCH CUBES
3 LARGE TOMATOES, PEELED AND QUARTERED
1 BAY LEAF
⅛ CUP CHOPPED FRESH THYME
¼ CUP CHOPPED FRESH PARSLEY
SALT AND FRESHLY GROUND BLACK PEPPER TO TASTE
COOKED WHITE RICE, FOR GARNISH

In a large soup pot, melt the margarine and sauté the onion, chili pepper, and okra until lightly browned. Reduce heat and simmer, covered, for 30 minutes, stirring occasionally.

Add the *Chicken Broth*, ham, and tomatoes. Tie the bay leaf, thyme, and parsley in a cheesecloth bag and add to the soup pot. Simmer, covered, for 30 minutes. Discard the cheesecloth bag. Add the salt and pepper.

Garnish each serving with the rice and serve.

Stews

Beef Stew

Yield: 1½ quarts

4 TABLESPOONS UNBLEACHED ALL-PURPOSE FLOUR
SALT AND FRESHLY GROUND BLACK PEPPER TO TASTE
1½ POUNDS LEAN BEEF CHUCK, CUT INTO 1½-INCH CUBES
3 TABLESPOONS VEGETABLE OIL
3 CUPS WATER
1 TABLESPOON WORCESTERSHIRE SAUCE
2 MEDIUM ONIONS, CHOPPED
6 SMALL CARROTS, CUT INTO 3-INCH PIECES
4 SMALL POTATOES
½ POUND GREEN BEANS, TOPPED, TAILED, AND CUT
    INTO 1-INCH PIECES
¼ CUP CHOPPED FRESH PARSLEY
1 BAY LEAF
½ TEASPOON CELERY SEEDS
SALT AND FRESHLY GROUND BLACK PEPPER TO TASTE
3 TABLESPOONS UNBLEACHED ALL-PURPOSE FLOUR
½ CUP COLD WATER

In a small bowl, combine the 4 tablespoons flour, salt, and pepper. Dredge the beef in the flour mixture.

In a large soup pot, heat the oil and brown the beef. Drain off the fat. Add the 3 cups water and Worcestershire sauce. Simmer, covered, for 1 hour, or until the meat is tender. Add the onions, carrots, whole potatoes, green beans, parsley, bay leaf, celery seeds, salt, and pepper. Simmer, covered, for 30 minutes more, or until the vegetables are tender. Remove the bay leaf and discard.

In a small bowl, blend the 3 tablespoons flour with the cold water to make a thin paste. Add the paste to the soup pot and cook until thickened, stirring frequently. Serve.

Tomato & Beef Stew

Yield: 1½ quarts

4 TABLESPOONS UNBLEACHED ALL-PURPOSE FLOUR
SALT AND FRESHLY GROUND BLACK PEPPER TO TASTE
2 POUNDS LEAN BEEF, CUT INTO 1½-INCH CUBES
3 TABLESPOONS VEGETABLE OIL
4 CUPS TOMATO JUICE OR PUREE
6 SMALL ONIONS
6 SMALL CARROTS
6 SMALL POTATOES
SALT AND FRESHLY GROUND BLACK PEPPER TO TASTE
2 TABLESPOONS UNBLEACHED ALL-PURPOSE FLOUR
2 TABLESPOONS COLD WATER

In a small bowl, combine the 4 tablespoons flour, salt, and pepper. Dredge the beef in the flour mixture.

In a large soup pot, heat the oil and brown the beef. Drain off the fat. Add the tomato juice. Simmer, covered, for 1 hour, or until the meat is tender. Add the whole onions, whole carrots, whole potatoes, salt, and pepper. Simmer, covered, for 45 minutes, or until the vegetables are tender.

In a small bowl, blend the 2 tablespoons flour with the cold water to make a thin paste. Add the paste to the soup pot and cook until thickened, stirring frequently. Serve.

Beef & Cheese Stew

Yield: 1½ quarts

2 CUPS COOKED BEEF ROAST, CUT INTO 1-INCH CUBES
1 CUP CHOPPED POTATOES
1 TABLESPOON CHOPPED ONIONS
1 TABLESPOON CHOPPED GREEN BELL PEPPER
1 SMALL CARROT, CHOPPED
3 TABLESPOONS CHOPPED GREEN CABBAGE
3 TABLESPOONS CHOPPED FRESH PARSLEY
1 QUART *BROWN STOCK* (SEE PAGE 11)
SALT AND FRESHLY GROUND BLACK PEPPER TO TASTE
2 TABLESPOONS UNBLEACHED ALL-PURPOSE FLOUR
2 TABLESPOONS COLD WATER
½ CUP GRATED LOW-FAT CHEDDAR CHEESE
GROUND PAPRIKA, FOR GARNISH

In a large soup pot, cover the beef, potatoes, onions, green pepper, carrot, cabbage, and parsley with the *Brown Stock*. Simmer, covered, for 30 minutes, or until the vegetables are tender. Add the salt and pepper.

In a small bowl, blend the flour with the cold water to make a thin paste. Add the paste to the soup pot and cook until thickened, stirring frequently. Add the cheese and stir until the cheese is melted.

Garnish each serving with the paprika and serve.

Hungarian Stew

Yield: 2 quarts

4 TABLESPOONS UNBLEACHED ALL-PURPOSE FLOUR
SALT AND FRESHLY GROUND BLACK PEPPER TO TASTE
2 POUNDS LEAN BEEF, CUT INTO 1½-INCH CUBES
3 TABLESPOONS VEGETABLE OIL
1 MEDIUM ONION, CHOPPED
1 TEASPOON CARAWAY SEEDS
½ TEASPOON GROUND HUNGARIAN PAPRIKA OR TO TASTE
2 CUPS WATER
3 CUPS DRAINED SAUERKRAUT
SALT AND FRESHLY GROUND BLACK PEPPER TO TASTE
1 CUP LOW-FAT SOUR CREAM

In a small bowl, combine the flour, salt, and pepper. Dredge the beef in the flour mixture.

In a large soup pot, heat the oil and brown the beef. Drain off the fat. Add the onion, caraway seeds, paprika, water, sauerkraut, salt, and pepper. Simmer, covered, for 1 hour, or until the meat is tender.

Before serving, add the sour cream and blend well. Serve.

Bavarian Stew

Yield: 1½ quarts

4 TABLESPOONS VEGETABLE OIL

2 POUNDS LEAN BEEF CHUCK, CUT INTO 1½-INCH CUBES

2 CUPS WATER

¾ CUP WHITE VINEGAR

3 LARGE ONIONS, SLICED

½ TEASPOON GROUND CLOVES

SALT AND FRESHLY GROUND BLACK PEPPER TO TASTE

3 TABLESPOONS UNBLEACHED ALL-PURPOSE FLOUR

1½ CUPS UNBLEACHED ALL-PURPOSE FLOUR

3 TEASPOONS BAKING POWDER

¾ TEASPOON SALT

¾ CUP LOW-FAT MILK

In a large soup pot, heat 2 tablespoons oil and brown the beef. Drain off the fat. Add the water, vinegar, and onions. Simmer, covered, for 1½ hours, or until the meat is tender. Add the cloves, salt, and pepper. Simmer, covered, for 20 minutes more.

In a small bowl, blend the 3 tablespoons flour with 2–3 tablespoons soup liquid to make a thin paste. Add the paste to the soup pot and cook until thickened, stirring frequently.

In a large bowl, sift together the 1½ cups flour, baking powder, and the ¾ teaspoon salt. In a small bowl, blend together the milk and the remaining oil. Add the milk mixture to the flour mixture, all at once, stirring quickly to form a soft dough.

Drop the dough by spoonful on the hot soup. Simmer, covered, for 15 minutes without removing the cover. Serve.

Danish Stew

Yield: 1½ quarts

4 TABLESPOONS UNBLEACHED ALL-PURPOSE FLOUR
SALT AND FRESHLY GROUND BLACK PEPPER TO TASTE
1½ POUNDS ROUND BEEF STEAK, CUT INTO 1½-INCH SQUARES
3 TABLESPOONS VEGETABLE OIL
1 SMALL ONION, SLICED
½ TEASPOON SUGAR
3 TABLESPOONS FRESH LEMON JUICE
3 CUPS HOT WATER
4 MEDIUM POTATOES, CUT INTO 1½-INCH CUBES
SALT AND FRESHLY GROUND BLACK PEPPER TO TASTE

In a small bowl, combine the flour, salt, and pepper. Dredge the beef in the flour mixture.

In a large soup pot, heat the oil and brown the beef and onion. Drain off the fat. In another small bowl, mix together the sugar and lemon juice and add to the soup pot. Simmer for 3–4 minutes. Add the hot water. Simmer, covered, for 1 hour, or until the meat is tender.

Add the potatoes, salt, and pepper. Simmer, covered, for 30 minutes, or until the potatoes are tender. Serve.

Dutch Stew

Yield: 1½ quarts

4 TABLESPOONS UNBLEACHED ALL-PURPOSE FLOUR

SALT AND FRESHLY GROUND BLACK PEPPER TO TASTE

½ POUND LEAN BEEF, CUT INTO 1-INCH CUBES

½ POUND LEAN PORK, CUT INTO 1-INCH CUBES

½ POUND BEEF LIVER, CUT INTO 1-INCH CUBES

3 TABLESPOONS VEGETABLE OIL

2 SMALL ONIONS, SLICED

2 QUARTS WATER

1 TABLESPOON WORCESTERSHIRE SAUCE

¼ CUP UNBLEACHED ALL-PURPOSE FLOUR

¼ CUP COLD WATER

SALT AND FRESHLY GROUND BLACK PEPPER TO TASTE

1½ CUPS UNBLEACHED ALL-PURPOSE FLOUR

3 TEASPOONS BAKING POWDER

1 TEASPOON SALT

¾ CUP LOW-FAT MILK

¼ CUP VEGETABLE OIL

In a small bowl, combine the 4 tablespoons flour, salt, and pepper. Dredge all the meat in the flour mixture.

In a large soup pot, heat the 3 tablespoons oil and brown the meat. Add the onions and sauté for 5 minutes, stirring frequently. Drain off the fat. Add the water and Worcestershire sauce. Simmer, covered, for 1½ hours, or until the meat is tender.

In a small bowl, blend the ¼ cup flour with the cold water to make a thin paste. Add the paste, salt, and pepper to the soup pot and cook until thickened, stirring frequently.

In a large bowl, sift together the 1½ cups flour, baking powder, and the 1 teaspoon salt. In a small bowl, blend together the milk and the ¼ cup oil. Add the milk mixture to the flour mixture, all at once, stirring quickly to form a soft dough.

Drop the dough by spoonsful on the hot soup. Simmer, covered, for 15 minutes, without removing the cover. Serve.

Hotch Potch Stew

Yield: 3 quarts

1 POUND LEAN BEEF, CUT INTO 1-INCH CUBES
1 POUND LEAN LAMB, CUT INTO 1-INCH CUBES
4 QUARTS COLD WATER
SALT AND FRESHLY GROUND BLACK PEPPER TO TASTE
1 CUP CHOPPED GREEN BEANS
2 MEDIUM CARROTS, CHOPPED
2 MEDIUM ONIONS, CHOPPED
2 STALKS CELERY, CHOPPED
2 MEDIUM TURNIPS, CHOPPED
½ CUP FRESH OR FROZEN PEAS
1 SMALL HEAD CAULIFLOWER, CUT INTO SMALL PIECES
½ SMALL HEAD LETTUCE, SHREDDED

In a large soup pot, cover the beef and lamb with the cold water. Let stand for 1 hour. Simmer, covered, for 2–3 hours.

Remove the meat and set aside. Strain the broth into a shallow container and chill to congeal fat. Lift off hardened fat and discard. Return the broth to the soup pot.

Add the reserved meat to the broth. Add the salt, pepper, green beans, carrots, onions, celery, and turnips. Simmer for 20 minutes, or until the vegetables are barely tender. Add the peas, cauliflower, and lettuce and simmer for 10–15 minutes more. Add water to thin, if necessary. Serve.

Irish Stew

Yield: 1½ quarts

2 POUNDS UNCOOKED CORNED BEEF

6 WHOLE PEPPERCORNS

1 TEASPOON GROUND MACE

1 TEASPOON CELERY SEEDS

¼ CUP CHOPPED FRESH PARSLEY

⅛ CUP CHOPPED FRESH MARJORAM

2 QUARTS WATER

2 MEDIUM POTATOES, SLICED

2 MEDIUM TURNIPS, SLICED

2 MEDIUM CARROTS, SLICED

1 MEDIUM ONION, SLICED

SALT AND FRESHLY GROUND BLACK PEPPER TO TASTE

3 TABLESPOONS UNBLEACHED ALL-PURPOSE FLOUR

2 TABLESPOONS WHITE VINEGAR

2 TABLESPOONS WATER

In a large soup pot, cover the corned beef, peppercorns, mace, celery seeds, parsley, and marjoram with the 2 quarts water. Simmer, covered, for 45 minutes. Strain the broth and taste. If too salty, discard the broth and replace with 2 quarts boiling water. Return the corned beef and the broth or water to the soup pot. Simmer, covered, for 1½ hours, or until the meat is tender.

Remove the corned beef and cut into 3-inch pieces. Return the meat to the soup pot. Add the potatoes, turnips, carrots, onion, salt, and pepper. Simmer, covered, for 30 minutes, or until the vegetables are tender.

In a small bowl, blend the flour with the vinegar and the 2 tablespoons water to make a thin paste. Add the paste to the soup pot and cook until thickened, stirring frequently. Serve.

Kidney Stew

Yield: 1 quart

2 SMALL BEEF KIDNEYS
2 CUPS COLD WATER
1 TABLESPOON FRESH LEMON JUICE
½ TEASPOON SALT
2 CUPS BOILING WATER
⅓ CUP UNBLEACHED ALL-PURPOSE FLOUR
SALT AND FRESHLY GROUND BLACK PEPPER TO TASTE
3 TABLESPOONS VEGETABLE OIL
3 TABLESPOONS CHOPPED ONIONS
6 SLICES LEAN BACON, COOKED AND CRUMBLED
HOT COOKED WHITE RICE
CHOPPED FRESH PARSLEY, FOR GARNISH

Split the kidneys and remove the membrane, fatty core, and veins. Rinse well and cut into ½-inch cubes. In a medium-size bowl, cover the meat with the cold water, lemon juice, and the ½ teaspoon salt. Soak for 30 minutes. Drain and rinse well with cold water.

In a medium-size saucepan, cover the meat with the boiling water. Simmer, covered, for 30 minutes. Drain on paper towels and reserve the cooking liquid.

In a small bowl, combine the flour, salt, and pepper. Dredge the meat in the flour mixture. In a large saucepan, heat the oil and brown the meat and onions. Add the bacon, the remaining flour from dredging, and the reserved cooking liquid and cook until thickened, stirring frequently.

Serve over the hot rice and garnish each serving with the parsley.

Chicken & Dumpling Stew

Yield: 1½ quarts

5 TABLESPOONS VEGETABLE OIL

ONE 3–4-POUND STEWING CHICKEN, CUT UP

1 MEDIUM ONION, CHOPPED

1 CLOVE GARLIC, MINCED

2 CUPS TOMATO JUICE OR PUREE

2 CUPS WATER

SALT AND FRESHLY GROUND BLACK PEPPER TO TASTE

2 CUPS FRESH OR FROZEN PEAS

3 TABLESPOONS UNBLEACHED ALL-PURPOSE FLOUR

½ CUP COLD WATER

2 CUPS UNBLEACHED ALL-PURPOSE FLOUR

4 TEASPOONS BAKING POWDER

1 TEASPOON SALT

1 CUP LOW-FAT MILK

In a large soup pot, heat 3 tablespoons oil and brown the chicken parts. Add the onion and garlic and sauté for 5 minutes, stirring frequently. Drain off the fat. Add the tomato juice and 2 cups water. Simmer, covered, for 2–2½ hours, or until the chicken is tender.

Remove the chicken and set aside. Strain the broth into a shallow container and chill to congeal fat. Lift off hardened fat and discard. Return the broth to the soup pot.

Remove the skin and bones from the reserved chicken and discard. Cut the meat into bite-size pieces and add to the soup pot. Add the salt, pepper, and peas and simmer for 10 minutes.

In a small bowl, blend the 3 tablespoons flour with the cold water to make a thin paste. Add the paste to the soup pot and cook until thickened, stirring frequently.

In a large bowl, sift together the 2 cups flour, baking powder, and 1 teaspoon salt. In a small bowl, blend together the milk and the remaining oil. Add the milk mixture to the flour mixture, all at once, stirring quickly to form a soft dough.

Drop the dough by spoonsful on the hot soup. Simmer, covered, for 15 minutes, without removing the cover. Serve.

Creole Stew

Yield: 2 quarts

ONE 4-5-POUND STEWING CHICKEN, CUT UP
2 QUARTS WATER
2 MEDIUM GREEN BELL PEPPERS, CORED, SEEDED, AND
   CHOPPED
1 MEDIUM ONION, CHOPPED
½ POUND COOKED HAM, CUT INTO 1½-INCH CUBES
2 CUPS CHOPPED TOMATOES
SALT AND FRESHLY GROUND BLACK PEPPER TO TASTE
2 CUPS FRESH OR FROZEN PEAS

In a large soup pot, cover the chicken parts with the water. Simmer, covered, for 2–2½ hours, or until the chicken is tender.

Remove the chicken and set aside. Strain the broth into a shallow container and chill to congeal fat. Lift off hardened fat and discard. Return the broth to the soup pot.

Remove the skin and bones from the reserved chicken and discard. Cut the meat into bite-size pieces and add to the soup pot. Add the green peppers, onion, ham, and tomatoes. Simmer, covered, for 30 minutes, or until the vegetables are tender.

Add the salt, pepper, and peas. Simmer for 10 minutes. Serve.

Brunswick Stew

Yield: 2 quarts

ONE 3–4-POUND STEWING CHICKEN, CUT UP

1 MEDIUM ONION, CHOPPED

2 QUARTS WATER

SALT AND FRESHLY GROUND BLACK PEPPER TO TASTE

¼ TEASPOON DRIED THYME

1 BAY LEAF

2 MEDIUM TOMATOES, CHOPPED

2 CUPS COOKED LIMA BEANS

1 CUP FRESH OR FROZEN WHOLE KERNEL CORN

1 CUP SLICED OKRA

2 TABLESPOONS UNBLEACHED ALL-PURPOSE FLOUR

2 TABLESPOONS COLD WATER

In a large soup pot, cover the chicken parts and onion with the 2 quarts water. Simmer, covered, for 2–2½ hours, or until the chicken is tender.

Remove the chicken and set aside. Strain the broth into a shallow container and chill to congeal fat. Lift off hardened fat and discard. Return the broth to the soup pot.

Remove the skin and bones from the reserved chicken and discard. Cut the meat into bite-size pieces and add to the soup pot. Add the salt, pepper, thyme, bay leaf, tomatoes, lima beans, corn, and okra. Simmer, covered, for 30 minutes. (If frozen or canned corn and okra are used, simmer for only 15 minutes.) Remove the bay leaf and discard.

In a small bowl, blend the flour with the cold water to make a thin paste. Add the paste to the soup pot and cook until thickened, stirring frequently. Serve.

Mulligatawny Stew

Yield: 2 quarts

2 TABLESPOONS VEGETABLE OIL

¼ CUP MINCED ONIONS

¼ CUP COOKED CHOPPED HAM

6 CUPS *CHICKEN BROTH* (SEE PAGE 20)

½ CUP COOKED DICED CHICKEN

⅓ CUP CHOPPED CELERY

2 CUPS COOKED CHOPPED TOMATOES

½ CUP CHOPPED APPLES

½ TEASPOON GROUND MACE

3 WHOLE CLOVES

1 TEASPOON CURRY POWDER

1 TABLESPOON CHOPPED FRESH PARSLEY

SALT AND FRESHLY GROUND BLACK PEPPER TO TASTE

DASH CAYENNE PEPPER

1 TABLESPOON TOMATO CATSUP

HOT COOKED WHITE RICE

LEMON SLICES, FOR GARNISH

In a large soup pot, heat the oil and sauté the onions and ham for 5 minutes. Add the *Chicken Broth*, chicken, celery, tomatoes, and apples. Tie the mace, cloves, curry powder, and parsley in a cheesecloth bag and add to the soup pot. Simmer, covered, for 1 hour, or until the vegetables and fruit are tender. Discard the cheesecloth bag.

Add the salt, pepper, cayenne pepper, and catsup. Stir well.

Serve over the hot rice and garnish each serving with a lemon slice.

Spanish Stew

Yield: 2 quarts

2 TABLESPOONS VEGETABLE OIL
2 POUNDS LEAN LAMB, CUT INTO 1½-INCH CUBES
2 QUARTS HOT WATER
1 MEDIUM ONION, CHOPPED
1 MEDIUM GREEN BELL PEPPER, CORED, SEEDED, AND CHOPPED
½ CUP UNCOOKED WHITE RICE
3 MEDIUM TOMATOES, PEELED AND QUARTERED
SALT AND FRESHLY GROUND BLACK PEPPER TO TASTE
1 EGG, BEATEN
1 TEASPOON VEGETABLE OIL
½ TEASPOON RED WINE VINEGAR

In a large soup pot, heat the oil and brown the lamb. Drain off the fat. Add the hot water. Simmer, covered, for 1–1½ hours. Add the onion, green pepper, rice, tomatoes, salt, and pepper. Simmer, covered, for 30 minutes, or until the vegetables are tender and the rice is cooked.

In a small bowl, blend together the egg, oil, and vinegar. Add the egg mixture to the soup pot and cook until slightly thickened, stirring frequently. Serve.

Lamb Stew

Yield: 2 quarts

4 TABLESPOONS UNBLEACHED ALL-PURPOSE FLOUR

SALT AND FRESHLY GROUND BLACK PEPPER TO TASTE

2½ POUNDS LEAN LAMB, CUT INTO 1½-INCH CUBES

¼ CUP VEGETABLE OIL

12 SMALL ONIONS

12 FRESH BUTTON MUSHROOMS

1 CLOVE GARLIC, MINCED

1 TEASPOON SUGAR

½ CUP CHOPPED FRESH PARSLEY

1 TABLESPOON WORCESTERSHIRE SAUCE

3 CUPS WATER

1 BAY LEAF

1 TEASPOON DRIED THYME

4 MEDIUM POTATOES, QUARTERED

6 MEDIUM CARROTS, CUT INTO 3-INCH PIECES

SALT AND FRESHLY GROUND BLACK PEPPER TO TASTE

3 TABLESPOONS UNBLEACHED ALL-PURPOSE FLOUR

½ CUP COLD WATER

In a small bowl, combine the 4 tablespoons flour, salt, and pepper. Dredge the lamb in the flour mixture.

In a large soup pot, heat the oil and brown the lamb. Remove the meat and add the whole onions, whole mushrooms, garlic, and sugar and sauté for 5 minutes, stirring frequently. Drain off the fat. Return the meat to the soup pot and add the parsley, Worcestershire sauce, and 3 cups water. Simmer, covered, for 30 minutes.

Add the bay leaf, thyme, potatoes, carrots, salt, and pepper. Simmer, covered, for 45 minutes. Remove the bay leaf and discard.

In a small bowl, blend the 3 tablespoons flour with the cold water to make a thin paste. Add the paste to the soup pot and cook until thickened, stirring frequently. Serve.

Oven Stew

Yield: 1½ quarts

2 TABLESPOONS VEGETABLE OIL

2 POUNDS LEAN LAMB, CUT INTO 1-INCH CUBES

1 MEDIUM ONION, SLICED

2 CUPS WATER

1 TABLESPOON WORCESTERSHIRE SAUCE

2 TABLESPOONS UNBLEACHED ALL-PURPOSE FLOUR

2 TABLESPOONS COLD WATER

SALT AND FRESHLY GROUND BLACK PEPPER TO TASTE

1 CUP FRESH OR FROZEN PEAS

3 MEDIUM CARROTS, SLICED

1 STALK CELERY, SLICED

Preheat oven to 325° F. In a large heavy skillet, heat the oil and brown the lamb. Add the onion and sauté for 5 minutes, stirring frequently. Drain off the fat. Add the 2 cups water and Worcestershire sauce. Bake, covered, for 1½ hours.

Remove the skillet from the oven. In a small bowl, blend the flour with the cold water to make a thin paste. Add the paste to the skillet and blend well. Add the salt, pepper, peas, carrots, and celery. Bake, covered, for 30 minutes more. Serve.

Rabbit Stew

Yield: 1½ quarts

1 RABBIT, CUT UP
2 CUPS DRIED LIMA BEANS
3 CUPS WATER
1 BAY LEAF
1 MEDIUM ONION, CHOPPED
6 MEDIUM CARROTS, SLICED
1 MEDIUM GREEN BELL PEPPER, CORED, SEEDED, AND CHOPPED
2 TABLESPOONS SOFT MARGARINE
2 TABLESPOONS UNBLEACHED ALL-PURPOSE FLOUR
SALT AND FRESHLY GROUND BLACK PEPPER TO TASTE

In a large soup pot, cover the rabbit parts and the beans with the water. Simmer, covered, for 2 hours. Add the bay leaf and onion. Simmer, covered, for 30 minutes more. Remove the bay leaf and discard.

Add the carrots and green pepper. Simmer, covered, for 30 minutes, adding more water, if necessary.

In a small saucepan, melt the margarine and blend in the flour. Gradually add 1 cup soup liquid and cook until thickened, stirring frequently. Add the soup liquid mixture to the soup pot. Stir well and reheat. Add the salt and pepper and serve.

Venison Stew

Yield: 1½ quarts

4 TABLESPOONS UNBLEACHED ALL-PURPOSE FLOUR
SALT AND FRESHLY GROUND BLACK PEPPER TO TASTE
2 POUNDS VENISON, CUT INTO 1½-INCH CUBES
3 TABLESPOONS VEGETABLE OIL
4 CUPS WATER
2 MEDIUM CARROTS, SLICED
½ CUP CHOPPED CELERY
1 MEDIUM ONION, SLICED
2 TABLESPOONS UNBLEACHED ALL-PURPOSE FLOUR
2 TABLESPOONS COLD WATER
1 TABLESPOON FRESH LEMON JUICE
SALT AND FRESHLY GROUND BLACK PEPPER TO TASTE

In a small bowl, combine the 4 tablespoons flour, salt, and pepper. Dredge the venison in the flour mixture.

In a large soup pot, heat the oil and brown the venison. Drain off the fat. Add the 4 cups water. Simmer, covered, for 1½ hours, or until the meat is tender. Add the carrots, celery, and onion. Simmer, covered, for 30 minutes more, or until the vegetables are tender.

In a small bowl, blend the 2 tablespoons flour with the cold water to make a thin paste. Add the paste to the soup pot and cook until thickened, stirring frequently.

Add the lemon juice, salt, and pepper and serve.

Oyster Stew

Yield: 3 quarts

SIX 8-OUNCE CONTAINERS FRESH OYSTERS
2 QUARTS *WHITE STOCK* (SEE PAGE 12)
2 TABLESPOONS SOFT MARGARINE
2 TABLESPOONS UNBLEACHED ALL-PURPOSE FLOUR
1 CUP HALF-AND-HALF
SALT TO TASTE
DASH CAYENNE PEPPER

In a colander, thoroughly rinse the oysters with cold water. Set aside.

In a large soup pot, add 6 cups *White Stock* and the reserved oysters. Bring to a boil. Reduce heat and simmer, covered, for 30 minutes.

In a medium-size saucepan, melt the margarine and blend in the flour. Gradually add the remaining *White Stock* and cook until thickened, stirring frequently. Add the stock mixture and half-and-half to the oyster mixture. Stir well and reheat. Add the salt and cayenne pepper and serve. **Note:** This soup should not be frozen.

Vegetable & Oyster Stew

Yield: 1½ quarts

TWO 8-OUNCE CONTAINERS FRESH OYSTERS
2 CUPS WATER
4 TABLESPOONS SOFT MARGARINE
2 MEDIUM CARROTS, CHOPPED
2 STALKS CELERY, CHOPPED
4 CUPS LOW-FAT MILK
1 CUP HALF-AND-HALF
SALT AND FRESHLY GROUND BLACK PEPPER TO TASTE
CHOPPED FRESH PARSLEY, FOR GARNISH

In a colander, thoroughly rinse the oysters with cold water. Set aside.

In a large soup pot, add the water and the reserved oysters. Simmer, covered, for 25 minutes.

In a medium-size saucepan, melt the margarine and add the carrots and celery. Cook the carrots and celery on low heat for 20 minutes, or until the vegetables are tender. Add the vegetable mixture, milk, and half-and-half to the oyster mixture. Stir well and reheat. Add the salt and pepper.

Garnish each serving with the parsley and serve. **Note:** This soup should not be frozen.

Chili

Texas Chili

Yield: 2 quarts

3 TABLESPOONS VEGETABLE OIL

3 POUNDS LEAN BEEF CHUCK, CUT INTO ¼-INCH CUBES

3–4 CLOVES GARLIC, MINCED

6 TABLESPOONS CHILI POWDER OR TO TASTE

2 TEASPOONS GROUND CUMIN

1 TABLESPOON GROUND OREGANO

3 TABLESPOONS UNBLEACHED ALL-PURPOSE FLOUR

2 QUARTS *BEEF BROTH* (SEE PAGE 21)

SALT AND FRESHLY GROUND BLACK PEPPER TO TASTE

CHILI POWDER, FOR GARNISH

HOT PEPPER SAUCE, FOR GARNISH

In a large skillet, heat the oil and brown the beef. Drain off the fat. Place the beef and garlic in a large soup pot.

In a small bowl, combine the chili powder, cumin, oregano, and flour. Sprinkle the flour mixture on the meat, stirring until well coated.

Add the *Beef Broth* and simmer, covered, for 2 hours, stirring occasionally. Skim off any foam. Add water, if necessary. Add the salt and pepper.

Garnish each serving with the chili powder and pepper sauce, if desired, and serve.

New Mexico Chili

Yield: 1 quart

¼ CUP VEGETABLE OIL
2 POUNDS LEAN BEEF, PORK, OR LAMB, CUT INTO 1-INCH
   CUBES
2 TABLESPOONS UNBLEACHED ALL-PURPOSE FLOUR
1 MEDIUM ONION, CHOPPED
2 CLOVES GARLIC, MINCED
6–8 SMALL MILD CHILI PEPPERS, SEEDED AND THINLY SLICED
2 SMALL HOT RED CHILI PEPPERS, SEEDED AND THINLY SLICED
1 TEASPOON GROUND OREGANO
¼ TEASPOON CUMIN SEED
2 CUPS *BROWN STOCK* (SEE PAGE 11)
SALT TO TASTE
COOKED PINTO BEANS

In a large skillet, heat 2 tablespoons oil and brown the beef. Drain off the fat. Place the beef in a large soup pot.

In the same skillet, heat the remaining oil and blend in the flour, onion, and garlic. Cook until the onions are lightly browned. Add the onion mixture, chili peppers, oregano, cumin seed, and *Brown Stock* to the soup pot. Simmer, covered, for 2 hours, stirring occasionally. Skim off any foam.

Add the salt and serve with the beans on the side.

Wyoming Chili

Yield: 1½ quarts

3 TABLESPOONS VEGETABLE OIL

1 CUP THINLY SLICED ONIONS

4 TABLESPOONS DICED GREEN BELL PEPPER

2 POUNDS LEAN BEEF, CUT INTO ½-INCH CUBES

3 CUPS BOILING WATER

1 CUP TOMATO JUICE OR PUREE

3 TABLESPOONS CHILI POWDER OR TO TASTE

¼ CUP COLD WATER

2 TEASPOONS SUGAR

3 CLOVES GARLIC, MINCED

4 CUPS COOKED RED KIDNEY BEANS

SALT TO TASTE

In a large skillet, heat the oil and sauté the onions and green pepper until the vegetables are tender. Add the beef and cook until browned. Drain off the fat. Place the onion mixture, beef, boiling water, and tomato juice in a large soup pot.

In a small bowl, blend the chili powder, cold water, sugar, and garlic to a smooth paste. Add the paste to the soup pot and stir well. Simmer, covered, for 1 hour, stirring occasionally. Skim off any foam. Add the beans and simmer, uncovered, for 1½ hours, stirring occasionally. Add the salt and serve.

California Chili

Yield: 1½ quarts

6 CUPS COOKED PINTO BEANS
4 CUPS WATER
6 TABLESPOONS VEGETABLE OIL
¼ CUP CHOPPED ONIONS
2 CLOVES GARLIC, MINCED
4 TABLESPOONS CHILI POWDER OR TO TASTE
1 TABLESPOON UNBLEACHED ALL-PURPOSE FLOUR
3 POUNDS LEAN BEEF, CUT INTO 1-INCH CUBES OR COARSELY
  GROUND
4 CUPS COOKED CHOPPED TOMATOES
1 TEASPOON GROUND OREGANO
SALT TO TASTE

In a large soup pot, combine the beans and the water. In a small saucepan, heat 3 tablespoons oil and sauté the onions and garlic until golden brown. Blend in the chili powder and flour. Add the onion mixture to the soup pot.

In a large skillet, heat the remaining oil and brown the beef. Drain off the fat. Place the beef in the soup pot. Simmer, covered, for 1 hour, stirring occasionally. Skim off any foam.

Add the tomatoes and oregano. Simmer, covered, for 1½ hours, stirring occasionally. Add the salt and serve.

Deep South Chili

Yield: 1½ quarts

3½ CUPS COOKED RED KIDNEY BEANS
4 CUPS WATER
¼ CUP VEGETABLE OIL
1 MEDIUM ONION, CHOPPED
1 CLOVE GARLIC, MINCED
1 MEDIUM GREEN BELL PEPPER, CORED, SEEDED, AND CHOPPED
3 POUNDS LEAN GROUND BEEF
1 POUND LEAN GROUND PORK
4 CUPS CHOPPED TOMATOES
1 TABLESPOON CHILI POWDER OR TO TASTE
1 TABLESPOON SUGAR
SALT AND FRESHLY GROUND BLACK PEPPER TO TASTE

In a large soup pot, combine the beans and the water. In a large skillet, heat the oil and sauté the onion, garlic, and green pepper until the vegetables are tender. Add the ground beef and pork and cook until lightly browned. Drain off the fat.

Add the meat mixture, tomatoes, chili powder, and sugar to the soup pot. Simmer, covered, for 2 hours, stirring occasionally. Add the salt and pepper and serve.

Midwestern Chili

Yield: 1½ quarts

2 TABLESPOONS VEGETABLE OIL
2 POUNDS LEAN GROUND BEEF
1 MEDIUM ONION, CHOPPED
1 MEDIUM GREEN BELL PEPPER, CORED, SEEDED, AND CHOPPED
2 TABLESPOONS CHILI POWDER OR TO TASTE
1 STALK CELERY, CHOPPED
4 CUPS TOMATO JUICE OR PUREE
2 CUPS COOKED RED KIDNEY BEANS
SALT AND FRESHLY GROUND BLACK PEPPER TO TASTE

In a large skillet, heat the oil and cook the ground beef, onion, and green pepper, sprinkled with the chili powder, until the vegetables are tender, but not browned. Drain off the fat.

Place the meat mixture, celery, tomato juice, and beans in a large soup pot. Simmer, covered, for 2½ hours, stirring occasionally. Add the salt and pepper and serve.

New York Chili

Yield: 2½ quarts

¼ CUP VEGETABLE OIL
4 POUNDS LEAN COARSELY GROUND BEEF
1 LARGE ONION, CHOPPED
2 CLOVES GARLIC, MINCED
1 TABLESPOON GROUND CUMIN
2 TABLESPOONS CHILI POWDER OR TO TASTE
3–4 DASHES HOT PEPPER SAUCE OR TO TASTE
1½ CUPS COOKED CHOPPED TOMATOES
8 CUPS WATER
SALT TO TASTE

In a large skillet, heat the oil and brown the ground beef, onion, and garlic. Drain off the fat.

Place the meat mixture, cumin, chili powder, pepper sauce, tomatoes, and water in a large soup pot. Simmer, covered, for 1½ hours, stirring occasionally. Add the salt and serve.

New England Chili

Yield: 1½ quarts

2 TABLESPOONS VEGETABLE OIL
½ CUP CHOPPED ONIONS
1 CLOVE GARLIC, MINCED
1 POUND LEAN GROUND BEEF
1 TABLESPOON CHILI POWDER OR TO TASTE
PINCH CAYENNE PEPPER OR TO TASTE
TWO 10¾-OUNCE CANS CONDENSED TOMATO SOUP
4 CUPS WATER
2 CUPS COOKED RED KIDNEY BEANS
SALT AND FRESHLY GROUND BLACK PEPPER TO TASTE

In a large skillet, heat the oil and brown the onions, garlic, and ground beef. Drain off the fat.

Place the meat mixture, chili powder, cayenne pepper, tomato soup, water, and beans in a large soup pot. Simmer, covered, for 1½ hours, stirring occasionally. Add the salt and pepper and serve.

Chili Peppers

Chili peppers, the ingredient for which chili was named and from which it derives its distinctive flavor, are grown on a small, compact plant much like the bell pepper and pimiento plants.

There are two varieties of chilies — hot and mild. A blend of both hot and mild chilies, dried, then ground to a powder, is the main ingredient of commercial chili powder. Chili powder also contains ground cumin seed and ground oregano.

Season recipes with hot chili peppers very carefully, adjusting the amount according to taste.

Vegetarian Chili

Yield: 1½ quarts

5 CUPS COOKED PINTO BEANS
3 CUPS WATER
2 TABLESPOONS VEGETABLE OIL
1 MEDIUM ONION, CHOPPED
2 CLOVES GARLIC, MINCED
¼ TEASPOON GROUND CUMIN
½ TEASPOON DRIED OREGANO
2 TABLESPOONS CHILI POWDER OR TO TASTE
2 CUPS TOMATO JUICE OR PUREE
SALT AND FRESHLY GROUND BLACK PEPPER TO TASTE
SOURDOUGH BREAD, THICKLY SLICED
GRATED PARMESAN CHEESE, FOR GARNISH

In a large soup pot, combine the beans and the water. In a small skillet, heat the oil and sauté the onion and garlic until lightly browned. Add the onion mixture, cumin, oregano, chili powder, and tomato juice to the soup pot. Simmer, covered, for 1½ hours, stirring occasionally. Add the salt and pepper.

Place one thick slice of the sourdough bread in each bowl. Pour the chili over the bread and garnish with the cheese. Serve.

Chilled Soups

Chilled soups are not suitable for freezing.

The best way to chill these soups is to chill them in the refrigerator for the specified time. For rapid chilling, however, place the soup in a bowl over cracked ice, or begin to chill the soup by putting it in the freezer for 10–15 minutes — no longer. Remove the soup from the freezer and continue chilling in the refrigerator. (Intense cold, if continued, destroys the texture of the soup.)

Consuela's Gazpacho

Yield: 1½ quarts

2–3 CLOVES GARLIC

3 CUPS TOMATO JUICE OR PUREE

2 TABLESPOONS OLIVE OIL

2 TABLESPOONS RED WINE VINEGAR

ONE 28-OUNCE CAN PLUM TOMATOES *OR* 6 LARGE TOMA-
TOES, CHOPPED

3 SMALL CUCUMBERS, PEELED AND CHOPPED

3 STALKS CELERY, CHOPPED

1 MEDIUM ONION, CHOPPED

4 TABLESPOONS CHOPPED FRESH PARSLEY

GARLIC CROUTONS, FOR GARNISH (SEE PAGE 214)

DICED CUCUMBERS, FOR GARNISH

In a blender or food processor, finely chop the garlic. Add 1 cup tomato juice, oil, and vinegar and process for 10 seconds.

Add *one half each* of the tomatoes, cucumbers, celery, onion and parsley. Process until the vegetables are coarsely chopped, *not* pureed. Transfer the vegetable mixture to a 2-quart container.

Repeat with the remaining tomato juice, tomatoes, cucumbers, celery, onion, and parsley. Chill for at least 1½ hours or until icy cold.

Garnish each serving with the croutons and cucumbers and serve.

Chilled Borscht

Yield: 2½ quarts

3 CUPS GRATED BEETS
2 QUARTS WATER
3 TABLESPOONS FRESH LEMON JUICE
1 TABLESPOON SUGAR
2 EGGS, WELL BEATEN
SALT AND FRESHLY GROUND BLACK PEPPER TO TASTE
LOW-FAT SOUR CREAM, FOR GARNISH

In a large soup pot, cook the beets in the water on medium heat for 15 minutes, or until the beets are tender crisp. Add the lemon juice and sugar. Let cool. Chill for at least 1 hour. Add the eggs and blend well. Add the salt and pepper.

Garnish each serving with a dollop of the sour cream and serve.

Vichyssoise

Yield: 1½ quarts

4 LARGE POTATOES, CHOPPED
2 SMALL ONIONS, CHOPPED
3 CUPS *CHICKEN BROTH* (SEE PAGE 20)
2 TABLESPOONS SOFT MARGARINE
2 CUPS LOW-FAT MILK
1 CUP HALF-AND-HALF
SALT AND FRESHLY GROUND WHITE PEPPER TO TASTE
MINCED FRESH CHIVES, FOR GARNISH

In a large soup pot, combine the potatoes, onions, and *Chicken Broth*. Simmer, covered, for 30 minutes, or until the vegetables are tender.

Puree the vegetables in a blender or food processor, or force through a metal colander or food mill. Return the vegetable mixture to the soup pot. Add the margarine, milk, half-and-half, salt, and pepper and blend well. Chill for at least 1 hour.

Garnish each serving with the chives and serve.

Cucumber Soup

Yield: 2 quarts

3 TABLESPOONS SOFT MARGARINE
2 LARGE CUCUMBERS, PEELED, SEEDED, AND CHOPPED
1 SMALL ONION, CHOPPED
1 QUART *CHICKEN BROTH* (SEE PAGE 20)
½ CUP LOW-FAT MILK
½ CUP HALF-AND-HALF
SALT AND FRESHLY GROUND WHITE PEPPER TO TASTE
CHOPPED FRESH DILL, FOR GARNISH

In a large soup pot, melt the margarine and sauté the cucumbers and onion until the vegetables are tender. Add the *Chicken Broth.* Simmer, covered, for 15 minutes.

Puree the vegetables in a blender or food processor, or force through a metal colander or food mill. Return the vegetable mixture to the soup pot. Add the milk, half-and-half, salt, and pepper and blend well. Chill for at least 1 hour.

Garnish each serving with the dill and serve.

Beet Soup

Yield: 1 quart

2 CUPS *BROWN STOCK* (SEE PAGE 11)
2 CUPS CLEAR BEET JUICE, FROM COOKED OR CANNED BEETS
2 TABLESPOONS ONION JUICE
½ CUP RED WINE
CUCUMBER SLICES

In a large saucepan, combine the *Brown Stock* and the beet juice. Bring to a boil and add the onion juice. Let cool. Chill for at least 1½ hours or until icy cold.

Add the wine and blend well. Place 2 or 3 cucumber slices in each bowl. Pour the soup over the cucumbers and serve.

Chilled Sorrel Soup

Yield: 1½ quarts

6 TABLESPOONS SOFT MARGARINE

6 MEDIUM LEEKS, CHOPPED (WHITE PART ONLY)

1 SMALL ONION, CHOPPED

2 CUPS CHOPPED FRESH SORREL

6 CUPS *CHICKEN BROTH* (SEE PAGE 20)

3 SMALL POTATOES, SLICED

1 CLOVE GARLIC, MINCED

½ CUP CHOPPED FRESH WATERCRESS

⅛ CUP CHOPPED FRESH THYME

⅛ CUP CHOPPED FRESH MARJORAM

¼ CUP CHOPPED FRESH PARSLEY

1 CUP HALF-AND-HALF

SALT AND FRESHLY GROUND BLACK PEPPER TO TASTE

CHOPPED FRESH CHERVIL, FOR GARNISH

In a large soup pot, melt the margarine and sauté the leeks and onion until transparent. Add the sorrel, *Chicken Broth*, potatoes, garlic, and watercress. Tie the thyme, marjoram, and parsley in a cheesecloth bag and add to the soup pot. Simmer, covered, for 45 minutes. Discard the cheesecloth bag.

Puree the vegetable mixture in a blender or food processor, or force through a metal colander or food mill. Return the vegetable mixture to the soup pot. Let cool.

Add the half-and-half, salt, and pepper and blend well. Chill for at least 1½ hours.

Garnish each serving with the chervil and serve.

Watercress Soup

Yield: 1 quart

2 CUPS CHOPPED FRESH WATERCRESS
3 CUPS *CHICKEN BROTH* (SEE PAGE 20)
4 TABLESPOONS SOFT MARGARINE
3 TABLESPOONS UNBLEACHED ALL-PURPOSE FLOUR
1 CUP LOW-FAT MILK
⅓ CUP HALF-AND-HALF
SALT AND FRESHLY GROUND BLACK PEPPER TO TASTE

In a large saucepan, combine the watercress and the *Chicken Broth.* Simmer, covered, for 20 minutes.

In a small saucepan, melt the margarine and blend in the flour. Gradually add the milk and cook until thickened, stirring frequently. Add the milk mixture, half-and-half, salt, and pepper to the large saucepan and blend well. Let cool. Chill for at least 1½ hours. Serve.

Buttermilk & Chicken Soup

Yield: 1 quart

4 CUPS CULTURED BUTTERMILK
1 SMALL CUCUMBER, PEELED AND FINELY CHOPPED
1 CUP COOKED FINELY CHOPPED CHICKEN
1 TABLESPOON CHOPPED CELERY LEAVES
1 TEASPOON PREPARED MUSTARD
SALT AND FRESHLY GROUND BLACK PEPPER TO TASTE
CHOPPED FRESH DILL, FOR GARNISH

In a large saucepan, combine all of the ingredients and blend well. Chill for at least 1 hour. Add the salt and pepper and beat the mixture well.

Garnish each serving with the dill and serve.

Spinach Borscht

Yield: 1½ quarts

1½ POUNDS FRESH SPINACH, FINELY CHOPPED

1 QUART WATER

¼ CUP SUGAR

1 TABLESPOON WHITE VINEGAR

2 TABLESPOONS FRESH LEMON JUICE

2 EGGS, WELL BEATEN

½ CUP LOW-FAT SOUR CREAM

SALT AND FRESHLY GROUND BLACK PEPPER TO TASTE

In a large soup pot, combine the spinach and the water. Simmer, covered, for 10 minutes. Add the sugar, vinegar, and lemon juice. Let cool.

In a small bowl, combine the eggs and the sour cream and blend well. Add the egg mixture to the cooled spinach mixture and mix well. Add the salt and pepper. Chill for at least 1½ hours or until icy cold. Serve.

Jellied Tomato Soup

Yield: 1 quart

1¾ CUPS COLD WATER

6 MEDIUM TOMATOES, CHOPPED

1 MEDIUM ONION, CHOPPED

2 STALKS CELERY, CHOPPED

1 SMALL GREEN BELL PEPPER, CORED, SEEDED, AND CHOPPED

1 TABLESPOON CHOPPED FRESH PARSLEY

4 WHOLE CLOVES

1 BAY LEAF

1 TABLESPOON UNFLAVORED GELATIN

SALT AND FRESHLY GROUND BLACK PEPPER TO TASTE

CHOPPED FRESH MARJORAM, FOR GARNISH

In a large soup pot, combine 1½ cups cold water, tomatoes, onion, celery, and green pepper. Tie the parsley, cloves, and bay leaf in a cheesecloth bag and add to the soup pot. Simmer, covered, for 20 minutes. Discard the cheesecloth bag.

Puree the vegetables in a blender or food processor, or force through a metal colander or food mill. Return the vegetable mixture to the soup pot.

In a small bowl, soften the gelatin in the remaining cold water. Add the gelatin mixture to the soup pot and stir until the gelatin is dissolved. Add the salt and pepper. Chill until firm. Arrange by spoonsful in each bowl.

Garnish each serving with the marjoram and serve.

Jellied Beef Soup

Yield: 1 quart

1 QUART *BROWN STOCK* (SEE PAGE 11)
1 TEASPOON WORCESTERSHIRE SAUCE
SALT AND FRESHLY GROUND BLACK PEPPER TO TASTE
1 BAY LEAF
1 WHOLE CLOVE
1 TEASPOON DRIED LOVAGE
2 TEASPOONS UNFLAVORED GELATIN
1 TABLESPOON COLD WATER
CHOPPED FRESH PARSLEY, FOR GARNISH

In a large soup pot, combine the *Brown Stock,* Worcestershire sauce, salt, and pepper. Tie the bay leaf, clove, and lovage in a cheesecloth bag and add to the soup pot. Bring to a boil. Reduce heat and simmer, covered, for 10 minutes. Discard the cheesecloth bag.

In a small bowl, soften the gelatin in the cold water. Add the gelatin mixture to the soup pot and stir until the gelatin is dissolved. Strain the soup liquid through three thicknesses of cheesecloth. Chill until firm. Arrange by spoonful in each bowl.

Garnish each serving with the parsley and serve.

Fruit & Sweet Soups

Fruit and sweet soups are not suitable for freezing.
Serve warm or chilled, never hot.

Berry Soup

Yield: 1½ quarts

2 CUPS BERRIES (RASPBERRIES, BLACKBERRIES, OR BLUEBERRIES,
    OR A COMBINATION)
3½ CUPS WATER
2 CUPS APPLE JUICE
DASH GROUND NUTMEG
SUGAR TO TASTE
2 TABLESPOONS CORNSTARCH
2 TABLESPOONS COLD WATER
¼ CUP FRESH LEMON JUICE
LOW-FAT WHIPPED TOPPING, FOR GARNISH

In a large soup pot, combine the berries and the 3½ cups water. Simmer, covered, for 20 minutes. Strain and set aside the berries. Return the liquid to the soup pot.

Add the apple juice, nutmeg, and sugar. In a small bowl, dissolve the cornstarch in the cold water and add to the soup pot. Cook until thickened, stirring frequently. Let cool. Chill for at least 1 hour. Add the reserved berries and lemon juice and blend well.

Garnish each serving with the whipped topping and serve.

Sour Cherry Soup

Yield: 2 quarts

2 POUNDS SOUR CHERRIES, PITTED
1½ CUPS SUGAR
2 CUPS WATER
2 TABLESPOONS CORNSTARCH
4 CUPS LOW-FAT MILK

In a large soup pot, combine the cherries, sugar, and water. Simmer, covered, for 20 minutes.

Puree the cherries in a blender or food processor, or force through a metal colander or food mill. Return the cherry mixture to the soup pot.

In a small bowl, dissolve the cornstarch in 2 tablespoons milk and add to the soup pot. Cook until thickened, stirring frequently. Add the remaining milk and blend well. Chill for at least 1 hour. Serve.

Coconut Soup

Yield: 2 quarts

2 CUPS GRATED COCONUT
2½ QUARTS WATER
½ CUP CORNSTARCH
¼ CUP COLD WATER
SUGAR TO TASTE

In a large soup pot, combine the coconut and the 2½ quarts water. Simmer, covered, for 1 hour. Strain and set aside the coconut. Return the liquid to the soup pot.

In a small bowl, dissolve the cornstarch in the cold water and add to the soup pot. Cook until thickened, stirring frequently. Add the reserved coconut and sugar and blend well. Cool slightly and serve.

Apple Soup

Yield: 2½ quarts

1½ POUNDS TART APPLES, CORED AND QUARTERED
1 STICK CINNAMON
PEEL OF ½ LEMON
2½ QUARTS WATER
5 TABLESPOONS CORNSTARCH
2 TABLESPOONS COLD WATER
6 TABLESPOONS DRY WHITE WINE OR TO TASTE
SUGAR TO TASTE
LOW-FAT WHIPPED TOPPING, FOR GARNISH

In a large soup pot, cook the apples, cinnamon stick, and lemon peel in 1 quart water on medium heat for 35 minutes, or until the apples are soft. Remove the cinnamon stick and discard.

Puree the apples in a blender or food processor, or force through a metal colander or food mill. Return the apple mixture to the soup pot.

Add the remaining water and reheat. In a small bowl, dissolve the cornstarch in the cold water and add to the soup pot. Cook until thickened, stirring frequently. Add the wine and sugar. Cool slightly.

Garnish each serving with the whipped topping and serve.

Prune Soup

Yield: 2 quarts

2½ CUPS DRIED PRUNES
½ CUP SUGAR
GRATED PEEL OF ½ LEMON
6 CUPS WATER
¼ CUP CORNSTARCH
3 CUPS LOW-FAT MILK

In a large soup pot, cook the prunes, sugar, lemon peel, and water on medium heat for 35 minutes, or until the prunes are very soft.

Puree the prunes in a blender or food processor, or force through a metal colander or food mill. Return the prune mixture to the soup pot.

In a small bowl, dissolve the cornstarch in 2 tablespoons milk and add to the soup pot. Cook until thickened, stirring frequently. Add the remaining milk and blend well. Cool slightly and serve.

Dried Fruit Soup

Yield: 2 quarts

¼ POUND DRIED PRUNES
¼ POUND DRIED APRICOTS
½ POUND DRIED APPLES
¼ POUND CURRANTS
¼ POUND RAISINS
2 QUARTS COLD WATER
¼ CUP QUICK-COOKING TAPIOCA
1 STICK CINNAMON
2 CUPS APPLE JUICE
2 TABLESPOONS SUGAR
GRATED PEEL OF ½ LEMON

In a large soup pot, soak the dried fruits overnight in the cold water. Do *not* drain. Add the tapioca and cinnamon stick. Simmer, covered, for 1½ hours. Remove the cinnamon stick and discard.

Puree the fruits in a blender or food processor, or force through a metal colander or food mill. Return the fruit mixture to the soup pot.

Add the apple juice, sugar, and lemon peel and blend well. Chill for at least 1 hour or until icy cold. Serve.

Pumpkin Soup

Yield: 1½ quarts

3 CUPS PUMPKIN, CUT INTO 1-INCH CUBES
1 TABLESPOON SUGAR
1½ CUPS WATER
3 CUPS LOW-FAT MILK
SALT TO TASTE
¼ TEASPOON GROUND CINNAMON
DASH GROUND NUTMEG
3 TABLESPOONS SOFT MARGARINE

In a large soup pot, cook the pumpkin and sugar in the water on medium heat for 40 minutes, or until the pumpkin is tender. Add more water, if necessary.

Puree the pumpkin in a blender or food processor, or force through a metal colander or food mill. Return the pumpkin mixture to the soup pot.

In a large saucepan, scald the milk and add to the soup pot. Stir well and reheat. Add the salt, cinnamon, nutmeg, and margarine and blend well. Cool slightly and serve.

White Wine Soup

Yield: 1 quart

1 TABLESPOON CORNSTARCH
4 TABLESPOONS SUGAR
SALT TO TASTE
DASH GROUND NUTMEG
3 EGG YOLKS, BEATEN
2 CUPS BOILING WATER
2 LEMON SLICES
2 CUPS SLIGHTLY SWEET WHITE WINE
LOW-FAT WHIPPED TOPPING, FOR GARNISH

In a large saucepan, combine the cornstarch, sugar, salt, and nutmeg. Add the egg yolks and blend well. Gradually add the boiling water, stirring constantly. Add the lemon slices. Simmer, covered, for 3–4 minutes. Add the wine and blend well. Cool slightly.

Garnish each serving with the whipped topping and serve.

Garnishes

If you use garnishes and other soup enhancers when you serve your delicious, homemade soup, your soup will be appealing to the senses of sight, taste, and texture. You can add variety and interest to any soup without adding appreciably to the cost or time. Most garnishes can be created in minutes from ingredients already on hand.

Place small amounts of the following on individual servings or tureens of soup to add contrast in color, texture, and taste.

For color:
Grated low-fat cheese
Unpeeled chopped red apples
Dollops of chili sauce
Sliced or chopped hard-cooked eggs
Thinly sliced lemons
Dash of ground nutmeg or cloves
Diced raw red or green bell peppers
Chopped fresh parsley
Thinly sliced stuffed green olives
Sliced red radishes
Low-fat sour cream or whipped topping, sprinkled with ground
    paprika
Cooked shredded carrots

For texture:
Toasted chopped nuts
Broken corn chips
Popcorn
Crushed potato chips
Cooked rigatoni or elbow pasta
Canned French-fried onion rings
Chow mein noodles
Cracker crumbs
Grated raw carrots or turnips

For taste:
Grated lemon or orange peel
Sautéed sliced mushrooms or onions
Chopped fresh chives or mint
Grated Parmesan cheese
Diced cucumbers
Chopped celery leaves

Flaked canned fish
Thinly sliced black olives

The following garnishes will add special interest to your home-made soups. Before serving, add the garnishes to the soup, or serve them on the side.

Almond Balls

24 ALMONDS, BLANCHED AND FINELY GROUND
½ CUP DRY BREAD CRUMBS
SALT TO TASTE
2 EGG WHITES, SLIGHTLY BEATEN
HOT VEGETABLE OIL

In a medium-size bowl, mix together the almonds, bread crumbs, salt, and just enough egg whites to bind together.

Shape the almond mixture into tiny balls and roll the balls in the remaining egg whites. Drop the balls, a few at a time, into the hot oil. Cook for 5 minutes or until golden brown. Drain on paper towels.

Fritters

1 EGG, VERY WELL BEATEN
1 TABLESPOON WATER
1 TABLESPOON FRESH LEMON JUICE
½ CUP UNBLEACHED ALL-PURPOSE FLOUR
SALT TO TASTE
HOT VEGETABLE OIL

In a medium-size bowl, mix together the egg, water, and lemon juice. Blend in the flour and salt.

Drop the mixture by teaspoonful into the hot oil. Cook for 3–4 minutes or until golden brown. Drain on paper towels.

Egg Balls

4 HARD-COOKED EGGS, CUT IN HALF

SALT TO TASTE

1 EGG YOLK, SLIGHTLY BEATEN

1 EGG WHITE, SLIGHTLY BEATEN

2 TABLESPOONS UNBLEACHED ALL-PURPOSE FLOUR

2 CUPS BOILING *CHICKEN BROTH* (SEE PAGE 20)

Remove the yolks from the hard-cooked eggs. Save the whites for use in other dishes. In a small bowl, mash the cooked egg yolks until smooth. Add the salt and enough of the raw egg yolk to make a dough.

Shape the dough into tiny balls and dip the balls into the raw egg white and then into the flour. Drop the balls, a few at a time, into the boiling *Chicken Broth*. Cook for 1–2 minutes or until firm. Drain on paper towels.

Cheese Puffs

¼ CUP GRATED LOW-FAT CHEDDAR CHEESE

4 TABLESPOONS UNBLEACHED ALL-PURPOSE FLOUR

½ TEASPOON GRATED ONIONS

SALT TO TASTE

DASH CAYENNE PEPPER

1 EGG WHITE, STIFFLY BEATEN

3 TABLESPOONS DRY BREAD CRUMBS

HOT VEGETABLE OIL

In a small bowl, mix together the cheese, flour, onions, salt, cayenne pepper, and egg white.

Shape the cheese mixture into small balls and roll in the bread crumbs. Drop the balls, a few at a time, into the hot oil. Cook, covered, until puffed and golden brown. Drain on paper towels.

Cheese Balls

¼ CUP SOFT MARGARINE
½ CUP COLD WATER
SALT TO TASTE
DASH CAYENNE PEPPER
⅛ TEASPOON GROUND PAPRIKA
¾ CUP UNBLEACHED ALL-PURPOSE FLOUR
3 EGGS
½ CUP GRATED LOW-FAT CHEESE (ANY TYPE)
HOT VEGETABLE OIL

In a medium-size saucepan, melt the margarine and add the cold water. Cook on medium heat for 2 minutes. Add the salt, cayenne pepper, paprika, and flour. Cook until the mixture forms a dough, stirring frequently. Cool slightly.

Add the eggs, one at a time. Add the cheese and stir well. Drop the mixture by teaspoonful into the hot oil. Cook for 1–2 minutes or until golden brown. Drain on paper towels.

Farina Puffs

2 TABLESPOONS SOFT MARGARINE
3 TABLESPOONS UNCOOKED FARINA OR CREAM OF WHEAT
   CEREAL
½ TEASPOON BAKING POWDER
1 EGG YOLK, WELL BEATEN
⅛ TEASPOON SALT
2 CUPS BOILING *BEEF BROTH* (SEE PAGE 21)

In a medium-size bowl, cream together the margarine, farina, and baking powder. Add the egg yolk and salt. Drop the mixture by ¼ teaspoonful into the boiling *Beef Broth*. Cook, covered, for 10 minutes or until puffed and golden brown. Drain on paper towels.

Matzo Balls

2 EGG YOLKS
3 TABLESPOONS VEGETABLE OIL
¾ CUP MATZO MEAL
½ CUP HOT *CHICKEN BROTH* (SEE PAGE 20)
½ TEASPOON SALT
2 EGG WHITES, BEATEN
2 CUPS HOT *CHICKEN BROTH*

In a large bowl, beat the egg yolks into the oil until well blended. Add the matzo meal, ¼ cup at a time, alternately with the ½ cup hot *Chicken Broth*. Add the salt. Chill for 1 hour.

Shape the mixture into small balls, adding more matzo meal, if necessary. Chill for 1 hour.

Roll the balls in the egg whites. Drop the balls, a few at a time, into the 2 cups hot *Chicken Broth*. Cook, covered, for 15–20 minutes or until golden brown. Drain on paper towels.

Rice Balls

1 CUP COLD COOKED WHITE RICE
2 TABLESPOONS UNBLEACHED ALL-PURPOSE FLOUR
1 EGG, BEATEN
SALT TO TASTE
DASH GROUND NUTMEG
1 TEASPOON GRATED LEMON PEEL
2 CUPS BOILING *CHICKEN BROTH* (SEE PAGE 20)

Puree the rice in a blender or food processor, or force through a metal colander or food mill. Place the rice in a medium-size bowl. Add the flour, egg, salt, nutmeg, and lemon peel.

Shape the mixture into small balls. Drop the balls, a few at a time, into the boiling *Chicken Broth*. Cook, covered, for 5 minutes or until slightly browned. Drain on paper towels.

Chicken Liver Balls

2 TABLESPOONS SOFT MARGARINE
¼ POUND CHICKEN LIVERS
1 TEASPOON FINELY CHOPPED FRESH PARSLEY
SALT AND FRESHLY GROUND BLACK PEPPER TO TASTE
4 EGG YOLKS
4 TABLESPOONS DRY BREAD CRUMBS
HOT VEGETABLE OIL

In a medium-size skillet, melt the margarine and sauté the chicken livers for 10 minutes.

Puree the chicken livers in a blender or food processor, or force through a metal colander or food mill. Return the chicken liver mixture to the skillet.

Add the parsley, salt, pepper, and enough egg yolks to make a firm mixture. Shape the chicken liver mixture into small balls and roll the balls in the bread crumbs. Drop the balls, a few at a time, into the hot oil. Cook for 5 minutes or until golden brown. Drain on paper towels.

Chicken Quenelles

½ POUND COOKED CHICKEN
2 TABLESPOONS SOFT BREAD CRUMBS
2 TABLESPOONS LOW-FAT MILK
2 TABLESPOONS SOFT MARGARINE
1 EGG, SLIGHTLY BEATEN
SALT TO TASTE
2 CUPS BOILING CHICKEN BROTH (SEE PAGE 20)

Grind the chicken in a blender or food processor. Set aside. In a medium-size bowl, soak the bread crumbs in the milk.

Puree the bread crumb mixture in a blender or food processor, or force through a metal colander or food mill. Set aside.

In the same bowl, add the reserved chicken, margarine, egg, salt, and enough of the reserved bread crumb mixture to make a firm mixture.

Shape the chicken mixture with two hot, moist spoons inverted over each other to form an *oval* ball. Gently drop the balls, a few at a time, into the boiling *Chicken Broth*. Cook, covered, for 5 minutes or until firm and golden brown. Drain on paper towels.

Oyster Forcemeat Balls

½ CUP FRESH OYSTERS
1 CUP WATER
1 TABLESPOON SOFT MARGARINE
½ CUP SLICED FRESH MUSHROOMS
½ CUP DRY BREAD CRUMBS
SALT TO TASTE
1 EGG YOLK, SLIGHTLY BEATEN

Preheat oven to 350° F. In a colander, throughly rinse the oysters in cold water. In a small saucepan, parboil the oysters for 3–4 minutes in the 1 cup water. Drain and finely chop the oysters. Set aside.

In a small skillet, melt the margarine and sauté the mushrooms for 5 minutes. In a medium-size bowl, combine the reserved oysters, mushrooms, bread crumbs, salt, and enough egg yolk to make a firm mixture.

Shape the mixture into small balls. Place the balls on a greased baking sheet. Bake for 5 minutes or until golden brown on all sides.

Forcemeat Balls

4 TABLESPOONS COOKED FINELY CHOPPED MEAT (BEEF, CHICK-
   EN, OR LAMB)
4 TABLESPOONS DRY BREAD CRUMBS
SALT AND FRESHLY GROUND BLACK PEPPER TO TASTE
1 TEASPOON CHOPPED FRESH PARSLEY
½ TEASPOON ONION JUICE
1 EGG YOLK, SLIGHTLY BEATEN
2 CUPS BOILING SEASONED BROTH (ANY TYPE, SEE PAGES 20–
   23)

In a medium-size bowl, mix together the meat, bread crumbs, salt, pepper, parsley, onion juice, and enough egg yolk to make a firm mixture.

Shape the mixture into small balls. Drop the balls, a few at a time, into the boiling broth. Cook, covered, for 5 minutes or until golden brown. Drain on paper towels.

Meat Dumplings

2 TABLESPOONS SOFT MARGARINE
2 CHICKEN LIVERS
1 MEDIUM ONION, FINELY CHOPPED
¾ POUND COOKED LEAN BEEF
2 EGGS
SALT AND FRESHLY GROUND BLACK PEPPER TO TASTE
1½ CUPS UNBLEACHED ALL-PURPOSE FLOUR
1½ TEASPOONS BAKING POWDER
⅛ TEASPOON SALT
¼ CUP VEGETABLE OIL
WATER

Preheat oven to 400° F. In a small skillet, melt the margarine and sauté the chicken livers and onion for 10 minutes, or until the chicken livers are cooked through and the onion is transparent. Cool slightly.

Grind the chicken livers, onion, and beef in a blender or food processor until slightly smooth. In a medium-size bowl, mix together the meat mixture, one egg, salt, and pepper.

In a large bowl, mix together the flour, baking powder, ⅛ teaspoon salt, remaining egg, and oil. Add enough water to make a dough. Roll out the dough ⅛ inch thick on a floured surface. Cut into rounds with a biscuit cutter.

Place 1 teaspoon of the meat mixture in the center of each round and fold the dough over to form a half moon. Pinch the edges together to seal. Pierce the tops of the dumplings with a fork and place on a greased baking sheet. Bake for 20–30 minutes.

Chestnuts in Consommé

24 CHESTNUTS, SHELLED AND BLANCHED
2 CUPS BOILING *BEEF CONSOMMÉ* (SEE PAGE 24)

Drop the chestnuts into the boiling *Beef Consommé.* Cook for 10 minutes, or until the chestnuts are barely tender. Drain on paper towels.

Bread Crisps

WHOLE WHEAT OR OAT BRAN BREAD SLICES
MELTED SOFT MARGARINE

Preheat oven to 300° F. Cut the bread slices into long narrow strips. Dip the strips into the margarine and place on a greased baking sheet. Bake until lightly browned on both sides.

Cheese Straws

1½ CUPS UNBLEACHED ALL-PURPOSE FLOUR
SALT TO TASTE
6 TABLESPOONS VEGETABLE SHORTENING
4 TABLESPOONS ICE WATER
1 CUP GRATED LOW-FAT CHEDDAR CHEESE

Preheat oven to 450° F. In a large bowl, mix together the flour and salt. Cut in the shortening until the mixture is granular. Stirring with a fork, work in just enough ice water to form a stiff dough.

Roll out the dough as thin as possible on a floured surface. Spread one half of the dough with the cheese. Top with the other half of the dough and roll out. Cut the layered dough into 3 by ½-inch strips and place on a greased baking sheet. Bake until golden brown on both sides.

Homemade Crackers

3 CUPS UNBLEACHED ALL-PURPOSE FLOUR
½ TEASPOON SALT
1 CUP SOFT MARGARINE
1 CUP LOW-FAT COTTAGE CHEESE

Preheat oven to 450° F. In a large bowl, mix together the flour and salt. Cut in the margarine and cottage cheese until the mixture forms a dough. Wrap the dough in wax paper and chill for at least 1 hour.

Roll out the dough ⅛ inch thick on a floured surface. Cut into different shapes with a knife or cookie cutter. Place the crackers on a greased baking sheet and pierce each cracker several times with a fork. Bake for 12–15 minutes or until lightly browned. Cool on a wire rack.

Whole Wheat Crackers

Use whole wheat flour (or one half whole wheat and one half unbleached all-purpose flour) in the *Homemade Crackers* recipe.

Caraway Crackers

Add 4 teaspoons caraway seeds to the mixture before chilling the dough in the *Homemade Crackers* recipe.

Poppy Seed Crackers

Top the crackers with poppy seeds before baking in the *Homemade Crackers* recipe.

Sesame & Onion Crackers

Add 4 teaspoons sesame seeds and 4 teaspoons grated onions to the mixture before chilling the dough in the *Homemade Crackers* recipe.

Herb Crackers

Add 4 teaspoons chopped fresh chives, parsley, or dill to the mixture before chilling the dough in the *Homemade Crackers* recipe.

Cornmeal Crackers

1 CUP YELLOW CORNMEAL
1½ TEASPOONS SUGAR
1 TEASPOON SALT
1 TEASPOON GRATED ONIONS
2 TABLESPOONS SOFT MARGARINE
¼ TEASPOON TABASCO SAUCE
1½ CUPS BOILING WATER
1 EGG WHITE, SLIGHTLY BEATEN

Preheat oven to 400° F. In a large bowl, mix together the cornmeal, sugar, salt, onions, margarine, and Tabasco sauce. Add the boiling water and stir until the water is absorbed.

Stir in the egg white. Drop the mixture by teaspoonsful on a greased baking sheet. Bake for 15 minutes or until lightly browned. Cool on a wire rack.

Cheese Crackers

HOMEMADE CRACKERS (SEE PAGE 211)
SOFT MARGARINE
GRATED LOW-FAT CHEESE (ANY TYPE)

Preheat oven to 350° F. Thinly spread the crackers with the margarine. Place the crackers on a greased baking sheet. Sprinkle the cheese on top of the crackers. Bake for 5 minutes, or until the cheese is melted and lightly browned.

Simple Croutons

DAY-OLD BREAD SLICES (WHOLE WHEAT, RYE, OR OAT BRAN)

Preheat oven to 250° F. Cut the crusts from the bread slices and cut the slices into cubes. Place on a greased baking sheet. Bake for 15 minutes or until golden brown on all sides.

Cheese Croutons

WHOLE WHEAT BREAD SLICES
SOFT MARGARINE
GRATED LOW-FAT CHEESE (ANY TYPE)

Cut the crusts from the bread slices. Spread the margarine on the bread slices and cut the slices into cubes. Place on a greased baking sheet and sprinkle the cubes with the cheese. Broil for 2–3 minutes, or until the cheese is melted and golden brown.

Garlic Croutons

WHITE OR WHOLE WHEAT BREAD SLICES
⅛ TEASPOON GARLIC POWDER OR TO TASTE
2 TABLESPOONS SOFT MARGARINE

Cut the crusts from the bread slices. In a small bowl, blend the garlic powder with the margarine. Spread the margarine mixture on the bread slices and cut the slices into cubes. Place on a greased baking sheet. Broil for 2–3 minutes or until golden brown.

Index

G

Garbanzo: garbanzo and noodle soup, 48
Gazpacho, 181
Giblets: giblet soup, 34
Gumbo: beef, 145; chicken, 143; chicken and oyster, 144; crab, 142; ham, 146

H

Ham: broth, 22; gumbo, 146; ham and artichoke soup, 47; ham and cabbage soup, 46; ham soup, 45; Mulligatawny stew, 161
Herb soup, 69
Herbs, 6

I

Ingredients, collecting, 5

K

Kidney bean. See Beans, dried
Kidneys: kidney stew, 157

L

Lamb: hotch potch stew, 155; New Mexico chili, 171; oven stew, 164; Scotch broth, 52; Spanish stew, 162; stew, 163
Leeks: leek soup, 59
Lentils. See Beans, dried
Lima bean. See Beans, dried
Liver: chicken liver balls, 205; Dutch stew, 154; mock turtle soup, 41
Lobster: bisque, 112; chowder, 131; soup, 122

M

Matzo balls, 204
Meatballs: bean and meatball soup, 83; meatballs and vegetable soup, 44
Minestrone, 50
Mushroom: cream of mushroom soup, 100; turkey and mushroom soup, 33

N

Navy bean. See Beans, dried
Noodles: beef and noodle soup, 36; chicken and noodle soup, 28; garbanzo and noodle soup, 48; tomato and noodle soup, 49
Normandie soup, 64

O

Onion: chowder, 139; cream of onion, 101; French onion soup, 59; onion soup, 60
Oxtail soup, 42
Oyster: bisque, 115; chicken and oyster gumbo, 144; chowder, 133; forcemeat balls, 207; stew, 167; vegetable and oyster stew, 168

P

Peanut: peanut butter soup, 104
Peas: bean and pea soup, 85; cream of pea soup, 105; pea and tomato soup, 87; split pea soup, 86
Pork: Dutch stew, 154; New Mexico chili, 171
Potage: red, 79